Child Molestation Bibliography

Also by Mary de Young

The Sexual Victimization of Children
(McFarland, 1982)
Incest: An Annotated Bibliography
(McFarland, 1985)

Child Molestation
An Annotated Bibliography

Compiled by
Mary de Young

McFarland & Company, Inc., Publishers
Jefferson, North Carolina, and London

Library of Congress Cataloguing-in-Publication Data

de Young, Mary, 1949–
  Child molestation.

  Includes indexes.
  1. Child molesting–Bibliography. 2. Child molesting
–United States–Bibliography. I. Title.
Z7164.S42D39 1987 [HQ71] 016.3627'044 86-27418

ISBN 0-89950-243-1 (sewn softcover; acid-free natural paper) ∞

Printed in the United States of America

McFarland & Company, Inc., Publishers
  Box 611, Jefferson, North Carolina

To John, Jill, and Stefanie

TABLE OF CONTENTS

ACKNOWLEDGMENTS

While spending the last year or so in the bowels of a half dozen different libraries, the little kindnesses of helpful people became particularly noteworthy. I would like to thank my sister, Karen Lorenski, for her assistance with the research, and my good friend, Linda Hertel Dykstra, Ph.D., for schlepping me to Kalamazoo, but mostly for her continuous support and encouragement.

The staffs of the various libraries were consistently helpful. I appreciated the assistance from the librarians at St. Mary's Hospital who ran a computer check on the medical references on child molestation, and the staffs of Grand Valley State College, Calvin College, Western Michigan University, Blodgett Memorial Medical Center, and Cooley Law School.

CHAPTER 1:
INTRODUCTION

Although historical evidence would suggest that child molestation has been, to some degree, a feature of every culture and each generation, only within relatively recent years has it been identified as a major social problem in this country. Case studies, empirical research, and theoretical approaches have appeared in the literature with increasing frequency in the last decade, and have demonstrated a growing interest in addressing this behavior from both a clinical and a conceptual perspective.

In recognizing the need for a comprehensive understanding of the origin, nature, dynamics and effects of this behavior, the purpose of this book is two-fold: to present the published references on child molestation in a manner that demonstrates they collectively form a body of scientific knowledge; and to organize those references in such a way that the various facets and dimensions of the behavior are clearly defined and illustrated.

References from social science, medical, and legal literature are cited in this bibliography to achieve these two purposes, so that the book has a distinctly clinical emphasis. Although there has been a wealth of material on child molestation published in popular magazines, pamphlets, brochures, and in-house manuals from a variety of different sources, as well as in literary and popular culture publications, these types of references are not cited in this book. The author recognizes that some of these references provide a unique slant or a rich illustration to the problem, but in order to maintain a clinical focus on child molestation that will be of use to mental health professionals, researchers, lawyers, medical personnel and policymakers, some of the "art" of bibliography has been sacrificed to its "science."

The definition of child molestation becomes the guide for the choice of which references are included in this annotated bibliography. Child molestation is defined as the exposure of a prepubescent child to sexual stimulation inappropriate for the child's age, psychological development, and psychosexual maturity, by a person at least ten years older, who may

1

either be unfamiliar to or acquainted with the child, but who is *not* related to the child by blood or legal means.

Some arbitrariness results from this definition since there is no standard definition of child molestation on which there is uniform consensus. The debate as to the exclusiveness of this sexual preference, as an example, is one aspect of the definition of child molestation on which there is little agreement; some of the cited references define child molestation as an exclusive sexual interest in children, while others view it as inclusive—that is, as a feature of a larger pattern of normative sexual behavior.

The chronicity of the behavior is another aspect of child molestation research that has sparked considerable debate, so that some of the cited references focus on samples of habitual child molesters while others include subjects who have engaged in that behavior only once while otherwise maintaining conventional sexual relationships with other adults. Requiring at least a ten year age difference between the child and the molester in the definition is somewhat discretionary and does exclude references that deal with sexual behavior between young peers.

Despite some arbitrariness, the definition used in this bibliography serves an important purpose in that it separates child molestation, as the term is used in this book, from incest, in which there is a relationship by blood or by legal means between the adult and the child. Since the latter has a thorough and comprehensive body of knowledge of its own, readers interested in surveying the literature on that topic are referred to the previously published *Incest: An Annotated Bibliography* (McFarland, 1985). Since the term "child molestation" often has been used in a generic sense, and since some studies mix incest with child molestation as it is defined in this book, the author had to exercise judgment as to which references could be included; those from which data on child molestation could not easily and clearly be culled were eliminated. This book also includes references on child sex rings and on child pornography since those two types of sexual exploitation also meet the guiding definition of child molestation.

A caveat on language must be included at this point. The literature variously refers to the behavior as "sexual victimization," or "sexual abuse"; to those who engage in the behavior as "pedophiles," "pedarasts," "sexual deviants," and "sex offenders"; and to the molested children as "victims." In an effort to be as value-free as possible, the term "child molestation" is used throughout the book; those who engage in the behavior are then referred to as "child molesters," and the children are simply referred to as "children." There is no attempt to be rhetorically manipulative in the choice of these terms; they are only used to create some degree of consistency in language throughout the book.

Even the most thoroughly researched annotated bibliography surely will overlook relevant sources, and this book is unlikely to be an exception. The author wishes to apologize in advance to those people who have contributed to our knowledge about child molestation but who, by oversight, are not included in this book. In the quest for brevity and objectivity, some of the content and "spirit" of the references may have been compromised; the author assumes all responsibility for any errors in judgment in the presentation of the literature. Finally, some references are repeated in this book because they deal with multiple facets of child molestation or because they can be cross-indexed in such a way as to illustrate different features of the behavior; consequently, the final number of references does not reflect the "true" count of references published on this topic.

This book is intended for busy lawyers, policy-makers, researchers, medical personnel and mental health professionals who require easy access to a large amount of data from a wide variety of sources. If it at all makes their important work a little bit easier, the purpose of this book will have been realized.

CHAPTER 2:
STATISTICAL STUDIES

There has been a considerable amount of debate as to the extent of child molestation in society. Since there is no uniform method for the collection of data, and since there is every indication from research studies and from anecdotal evidence that child molestation is an underreported behavior, no reliable figures as to its true incidence in the general population can be determined. The following studies examine its statistical incidence in select populations.

1. Baker, A.W. and Duncan, S.P. "Child Sexual Abuse: A Study of Prevalence in Great Britain." **Child Abuse and Neglect,** 9(4): 457-467, 1985.

A nationally representative sample of 2,019 residents of Great Britain were interviewed to determine the incidence of sexually abusive experiences during childhood. The 10% who report having had such experiences do not differ significantly from those who did not as far as social class and area of residence are concerned, but do tend to be younger, and are more likely to be female. The majority of those who report having been sexually abused state that the experience had a damaging effect on them.

2. DiVasto, P.V.; Kaufman, A.; Rosner, L.; Jackson, R.; Christy, J.; Pearson, S.; and Burgett, T. "The Prevalence of Sexually Stressful Events Among Females in the General Population." **Archives of Sexual Behavior**, 13(1): 59-67, February 1984.

A sample of 500 adult women in Albuquerque, New Mexico was given an anonymous questionnaire requesting demographic data and information on sexually stressful events in their lives. The latter reported incidents were grouped into nonevasive events (e.g. receiving obscene telephone calls, witnessing an indecent exposure), or invasive events (e.g. attempted rape, rape). A total of 416 sexually stressful events are reported by 376 women in the sample, 23% of whom were under thirteen years of age at the time. Slightly more than 50% of those incidents were perpetrated by strangers, and slightly less than 50% are classified as invasive events. Those childhood incidents of sexually stressful events that are invasive in nature are rated as the most emotionally unsettling by the responding women.

4

3.   Finkelhor, D. "How Widespread Is Child Sexual Abuse?" **Children Today**, 13(4): 18-20, July/August 1984.

There are no precise and reliable figures on the rate of child molestation, and even the most systematic efforts to collect such data are believed to seriously underestimate the extent of the problem. The data from a variety of self-report studies are reviewed to support this contention.

4.   Fritz, G.S.; Stoll, K.; and Wagner, N.N. "A Comparison of Males and Females Who Were Sexually Molested as Children." **Journal of Sex and Marital Therapy**, 7(1): 54-59, Spring 1981.

A 45-item questionnaire was given to 952 college students surveying all forms of early sexual experiences, demographic data, and current sexual behavior. The rate of reported molestation as children for the female students is 7.7%; for the males, 4.8%. Women who were molested as children are over twice as likely to report current problems with sexual adjustment than are the nonmolested women, and are much more likely to describe the molestation in negative terms than do the males who were molested as children.

5.   Gagnon, J.H. "Female Child Victims of Sexual Offenses." **Social Problems**, 13(2): 176-192, Fall 1965.

Twelve hundred college age females who are white and predominately middle class and who had earlier responded to the Kinsey Group survey on sexual behavior, were questioned about their sexual experiences as children. A total of 26% of the respondents report having had at least one sexual contact with an adult male before the age of thirteen; the mean age for the respondents at the time of the incident was 9.9 years old. Males were the aggressors in 98.5% of the cases reported by this sample. The vast majority of the women assessed the experiences as negative in their impact on their psychological well being.

6.   Gundlach, R.H. "Sexual Molestation and Rape Reported by Homosexual and Heterosexual Women." **Journal of Homosexuality**, 2(4): 367-384, Summer 1977.

A questionnaire regarding incidents of unwanted and/or coercive sexual molestation during childhood or adolescence was administered to 225 lesbian and 233 heterosexual women; 30% of the lesbian women and 21% of the heterosexual women report having had such experiences.

7.   Herold, E.S.; Mantle, D.; and Zemitis, O. "A Study of Sexual Offenses Against Females." **Adolescence**, 14(53): 65-72, Spring 1979.

An anonymous, closed-end questionnaire was administered to 103 female university students for the purpose of determining the rate of sexual victimization in that sample. A total of 9% of the students report having been sexually assaulted before the age of fourteen.

8.   Kercher, G.A. and McShane, M. "The Prevalence of Child Sexual Abuse Victimization in an Adult Sample of Texas Residents." **Child Abuse and Neglect**, 8(4): 495-501, 1984.

A random sample of 2000 names of people with valid Texas drivers licenses was mailed a questionnaire which inquired as to their opinions regarding child sexual abuse laws and the legal proceedings for dealing with identified cases; demographic information; and their personal history of sexual victimization as children. The 1,056 returned surveys report sexual molestation in the childhoods of 7.4% of the respondents. A disproportionate number of those respondents have annual incomes under $6,000, are currently over the age of fifty, and have less than a high school education. The molestation rate per 100 for white females is 9.8%; for black females it is 10.4%; and is 21.7% for Hispanic females. The molestation rate per 100 for white males is 3.4%; for black males it is 3%; and is 16% for Hispanic males. Small sample sizes preclude making generalizations about the prevalence of child molestation in ethnic minority populations.

9.   Landis, J.T. "Experiences of 500 Children with Adult Sexual Deviation." **Psychiatric Quarterly (Supplement)**, 30 (1): 91-109, 1956.

A questionnaire about childhood sexual experiences was administered to 1495 college students. Of the 1028 female respondents, 35% had been sexually molested as children by a family member or by persons who were not related to them. The mean age at the time of the molestation was 11.7 years and in each case, the perpetrator was a male. Of the 467 male respondents, 30% report childhood sexual experiences with adults; again, the rate of molestation by a non-family person is not separated out from the statistic. The mean age at the time of the molestation for males was 14.4 years, and in 84% of the cases, the perpetrator was a male. The degree of trauma experienced is related to the type of sexual molestation reported, with intercourse and attempted intercourse rated as more traumatic than exhibitionism; and to the degree of acquaintance between the child and the adult, with adults known to the children creating more trauma than those who are strangers. Finally, the more traumatic the behavior was, the less likely the child reported it to anyone.

10.   Russell, D.E.H. "The Incidence and Prevalence of Intrafamilial and Extrafamilial Sexual Abuse of Female Children." **Child Abuse and Neglect**, 7(2): 133-146, 1983.

A random survey of 930 women who were questioned by specially trained interviewers matched wherever possible to the age and ethnicity of the respondents, was conducted in San Francisco. Sexual molestation before the age of 18 was reported by 38% of the respondents.

11.   Sarafino, E.P. "An Estimate of the Nationwide Incidence of Sexual Offenses Against Children." **Child Welfare**, 58(2): 127-134, February 1979.

Based on child molestation reports from the state of Connecticut, Washington, D.C., and from the cities of Minneapolis and Brooklyn, it is extrapolated that 336,200 cases of child molestation were reported in this country each year. Acknowledging that the number of unreported cases is three to four times higher than reported cases, extrapolation would project a total of 1.3 million "true" cases of child molestation each year. Reported data show that 92% of the cases are heterosexual in nature. Data also show that a standardized reporting system should be implemented throughout the country.

12. Swift, C. "Sexual Victimization of Children: An Urban Mental Health Survey." **Victimology: An International Journal,** 2(2): 322-326, 1977.

Defining sexual victimization as rape; forced anal or oral intercourse; penetration of the oral, vaginal, or anal orifice with an object, or molestation, thirty mental health clinicians were surveyed to determine the amount of contact they had had with cases of this kind. The twenty respondents indicate that they have seen 74 cases of sexual victimization over a designated twelve month period of time, and that those cases involved recently molested children, adults reporting a childhood history of molestation, and adults who had molested children. Males constitute 33% of the mental health clients; although all clients show a low rate of reporting the molestation, the males demonstrate considerably more reticence in reporting.

13. Wolters, W.H.G.; Zwann, E.J.; Wagenaar-Schwencke, P.M.; and Deenen, T.A.M. "A Review of Cases of Sexually Exploited Children Reported to the Netherlands State Police." **Child Abuse and Neglect,** 9(4): 571-574, 1985.

Reports of child molestation reported to the nineteen offices of the state police in the Netherlands are analyzed. Most of the 106 cases involve children under the age of 12 who were involved in single incidents of fondling or masturbation. Threats and coercion to secure the cooperation of the child and to assure the secrecy of the behavior were used in approximately half of the cases. No special characteristics of the molested children emerge from the reports; neither is there any special aspect of their family lives. All of the molesters are male and gave a wide range of rationalizations for their behavior.

14. Wyatt, G.E. "The Sexual Abuse of Afro-American and White American Women in Childhood." **Child Abuse and Neglect,** 9(4): 507-519, 1985.

Structured interviews were conducted with 126 Black and 122 white women who were generally matched for socioeconomic level and age. An incidence of sexual molestation during childhood is reported by 57% of the Black women, and 67% of the white women. Analysis of the data shows that white females are more likely to have experienced molestation between the ages of six and eight, while Black women are more likely to have experienced it between the ages of nine and twelve. For both groups, the molester is most likely to be male and of the same ethnicity.

15. Wyatt. G.E. and Peters, S.D. "Issues in the Definition of Child Sexual Abuse in Prevalence Research." **Child Abuse and Neglect,** 10(2): 231-240, 1986.

Four recent studies on the prevalence of child sexual abuse are reviewed so that the impact of differential definitions on the findings can be assessed. The similarities and dissimilarities in definitions regarding the upper age limit of the subject, the criteria used to define a given sexual behavior as abusive, the inclusion or exclusion of sexual experiences involving peers, and the use of different criteria for sexual incidents occurring during adolescence are explored.

16. Wyatt, G.E. and Peters, S.D. "Methodological Considerations in Research on the Prevalence of Child Sexual Abuse." **Child Abuse and Neglect,** 10(2): 241-251, 1986.
Four recent studies on the prevalence of child sexual abuse are reviewed and the methodological differences in the studies are analyzed. The review shows that two aspects of data collection contribute the wide disparity in the findings of prevalence among these studies: the use of face-to-face interviews and the use of multiple questions asking about specific types of abusive sexual behavior are associated with higher prevalence rates. It is recommended that future surveys use broad and indirect descriptions of the research in the initial recruitment phase; that face-to-face interviews be conducted in private and comfortable surroundings; that the interviewers be trained and matched in ethnicity to the subject; and that the subject be reimbursed for her or his participation.

CHAPTER 3:
HISTORICAL CONSIDERATIONS

There is always a temptation to assume that a behavior that has been recently identified as a social problem is a product of the generation that labels it as such, but as compelling as that temptation is, it would also be wrong. There is a considerable amount of historical research that suggests that the sexual molestation of children has been a feature of each generation and culture; how it is defined, how the public reacts to it, and how it is treated varies with the social, cultural, religious, political and economic forces characteristic of that culture and that point in time, but its historical continuity is well demonstrated.

The following references examine child molestation within a historical context. It should be noted that many of them deal with homosexual child molestation, since the "double deviance" implied by that behavior has always evoked the strongest social and legal reaction.

17. Bentham, J. "Offenses Against One's Self: Paederasty." **Journal of Homosexuality,** 3(4): 389-405, Summer 1978. Part II found in **Journal of Homosexuality,** 4(1): 91-107, Fall 1978.
Written in 1785, this essay is the first known argument for homosexual law reform in England. The legal scholar and social reformer Jeremy Bentham advocates the decriminalization of sodomy that was punishable at that time by hanging. He argues that homosexual acts do not weaken men, threaten the institution of marriage or endanger the welfare of children, nor do they represent acts of heresy or witchcraft. Writing in a time of rampant homophobia, the essay confronts the antipathy to pleasure in general, and to sexual pleasure in specific, that Bentham argues was the cause of repressive legislation and discriminatory practices.

18. Burg, B.R. "Ho Hum, Another Work of the Devil: Buggery and Sodomy in Early Stuart England." **Journal of Homosexuality,** 6(1/2): 69-78, Fall/Winter, 1980/1981.

A review of handbooks for justices of the peace, sworn depositions, and other judicial records shows that 17th century English society was quite tolerant of homosexuality, although severe penalties existed in the law for homosexuals who molested male children. The levying of such penalties, however, was dependent on the social class and the political allegiance of the accused, a fact that is demonstrated in the case of Nicholas Udall, noted churchman, playwright, and headmaster who was removed from his teaching post but not prosecuted after having been accused of sodomy with his adolescent students.

19. Crompton, L. "Jeremy Bentham's Essay on 'Paederasty': An Introduction." **Journal of Homosexuality,** 3(4): 383-387, Summer 1978.
The great 18th century English legal scholar and social reformer, Jeremy Bentham's essay on pederasty is introduced. It is noted that Bentham left over 300 pages of thoughts on homosexuality and the law, and that his perception of male homosexuality is more akin to that of bisexuality in that he believed homosexuals could be convinced to marry. He also more liberally defines homosexuality as sexual attraction to both adult males and male adolescents.

20. Gilbert, A.N. "Buggery and the British Navy, 1700-1861." **Journal of Social History,** 10(1): 72-98, Fall 1976.
Historically, the military has reflected the attitudes and practices of the larger society; such congruity was found in the British Navy's reaction to homosexuality in the 18th century. The Navy's practice of conscripting young boys to work on the ships posed special problems in this area, so although the standard of evidence was high and the testimony of any boy who accused a sailor of sexual molestation was routinely doubted, once found guilty of sodomy, the sailors were given harsh punishments. Whippings were the most frequently used corporal punishments, with one case of 425 lashes given for a conviction of sodomy. Executions also occurred and it is estimated that 31% of all executions of British sailors between 1800 and 1816 were for sodomy convictions.

21. Oaks, R.F. "Things Fearful to Name: Sodomy and Buggery in 17th Century New England." **Journal of Social History.** 12(2): 268-281, Winter 1978.
In colonial America, sodomy referred to homosexual acts and buggery to bestiality, but on some occasions, and in some cases, the terms were used interchangeably. Both were punishable by death, reflecting the Old Testament prohibitions against such behavior, but the death penalty was rarely carried out since the scarcity of labor precluded executing deviant persons. The Humfrey case of 1641 is described in detail, since it was this case, in which three men sexually molested two young sisters over a several year period of time, that extended the law against sodomy to cases of child molestation.

22. Oaks, R.F. "Defining Sodomy in 17th Century Massachusetts." **Journal of Homosexuality,** 6(1/2): 79-83, Fall/Winter 1980/1981.

Reflecting Old Testament dictates, early colonial America established a law against sodomy and set the punishment as death. Although sodomy originally referred to homosexual acts between adults, its definition was expanded to include child molestation after the 1641 Humfrey case, in which three men were charged with sexually molesting two young sisters over a several year period of time; because the colony had no child molestation law, the men were convicted under the sodomy law. In the light of the lack of consensus about the merit of this approach, especially in the absence of any penetration and with no witnesses to verify the girls' stories, the three men were given corporal punishment instead of the death penalty.

23. Ruggiero, G. "Sexual Criminality in the Early Renaissance, Venice 1338-1358." **Journal of Social History,** 8(4): 18-33, Summer 1975.

Sexual crimes, and rape in particular, were viewed as relatively minor offenses in the early Renaissance. A review of court records in Venice, Italy shows that rape offenses against adults usually resulted in a sentence of one year in jail, while child molestation offenses usually resulted in a sentence of two years in jail. The political and economic realities of 14th century Venice life are discussed to offer reasons as to why such light sentences were given.

24. Taylor, B. "Motives for a Guilt-Free Pederasty: Some Literary Considerations." **Sociological Review,** 24(1): 97-114, February 1976.

The overt pederasty of poets like Oscar Wilde, Aubrey Beardsley, Algernon Swinburne, and Edward Cacroft Leroy is evident in their works. Several themes emerge in the poetry of these so-called "Uranian" poets, and each appears to justify and motivate their love of young boys. These themes include the transience of boyhood, lost youth, a divine sanction and a class sanction for pederasty, misogyny, and the erotic superiority of pederasty.

25. Taylor, K.J. "Venereal Disease in 19th Century Children." **Journal of Psychohistory,** 12(4): 431-463, Spring 1985.

Nineteenth century physicians only had a limited knowledge of the nature and extent of venereal disease, and usually did not regard sexual contact as the predominant mode of transmission. The cases of 381 children with venereal disease, gleaned from 19th century medical journals, show that doctors regarded the disease as originating from one of three sources: an unhealthy environment, from germs, or as a punishment from God. Challenges to these theories did not occur until late in the century, at which time the presence of venereal disease in children was viewed as symptomatic of sexual molestation.

26. Trumbach, R. "London's Sodomites: Homosexual Behavior and Western Culture in the 18th Century." **Journal of Social History,** 11(1): 1-33, Fall 1977.

A world ethnographic survey of homosexual behavior in the late 18th century is constructed by using the reports of European travellers as well as other random data. The taboo against homosexuality was consistent and strong throughout western culture and participants risked death if discovered. It was widely believed during this time that homosexuals preyed on young children and that belief, in part, justified both social stigma and severe legal penalties.

27.   Ungaretti, J.R. "Pederasty, Heroism and the Family in Classical Greece." **Journal of Homosexuality,** 3(3): 291-300, Spring 1978.

The system of pederasty was an accepted, socially endorsed sexual relationship between an older man and a young boy. Functioning primarily as an educational system for the boy, pederasty has its roots in the ancient Greek warrior tradition.

CHAPTER 4:
CLINICAL DESCRIPTIONS OF CHILD MOLESTERS

Clinical descriptions of child molesters abound in the literature. Using objective and projective personality tests, phallometric measures in response to various stimuli, case studies, and restrospective analyses of data, the following references attempt to describe the motivations, cognitions, emotions, and family backgrounds of child molesters.

Testing

The goal of most of the studies that administer objective or projective personality tests to samples of child molesters is to develop a psychological profile of a "typical" child molester. Since all of the following references use incarcerated, convicted, or hospitalized subjects who likely may vary in the chronicity and exclusiveness of their molesting behavior from those child molesters who are never arrested and convicted, the typicalness of the suggested profiles should be regarded cautiously.

28. Anderson, W.P. and Kunce, J.T. "Sex Offenders: Three Personality Types." **Journal of Clinical Psychology**, 35(3): 671-677, July 1979.
The MMPI profiles of 92 child molesters, rapists, and incestuous males were analyzed by Q-Factor Analysis and three major personality types emerge. The F,Sc (Frequency/Schizophrenia) Type is characterized by long-term, socially maladjustive behavior and by anxiety and depression. The D,Pd (Depression Psychopathic Deviate) Type is most likely to have a history of chronic borderline social adjustment, characterized by alcoholism and a prior criminal record. Child molesters are most likely to be of the Pd,Ma (Psychopathic Deviate, Hypomania) Type which shows the best adjustment.

29. Armentrout, J.A. and Hauer, A.L. "MMPI's of Rapists of Adults, Rapists of Children, and Non-Rapist Sex Offenders." **Journal of Clinical Psychology**, 34(2): 330-332, April 1978.

The MMPI scores of 13 rapists, 21 child molesters, and 17 minor sex offenders are compared. An elevation on scale 4 (Pd or Psychopathic Deviate scale) is noted for all of these groups, demonstrating that each is impulsive, pleasure-oriented, socially nonconforming, and unable to tolerate frustration. The elevations on scale 8 (Sc or Schizophrenia) differ significantly for each group, however. Child molesters have a primed 4-8 profile, suggesting that they are also hostile, avoid close emotional involvement, have poor judgment and low social intelligence. The rapists, with a primed 8-4 profile, are significantly more angry and alienated, while the minor sex offenders, with a 4-prime profile, show little hostility and resentment.

30.   Cowen, E.L. and Stricker, G. "The Social Desirability of Trait Descriptive Terms: A Sample of Sexual Offenders." **Journal of Social Psychology,** 59: 307-315, February 1963.

Using a 139-item list of trait descriptive adjectives, a group of 40 hospitalized child molesters is asked to use a 7-point scale to rate the social desirability of each adjective; results are compared to those of groups of alcoholics, schizophrenics, hospitalized controls, and college students. The child molesters differ significantly from every group except the alcoholics, and differ the most from the college students with respect to the mean level of the social desirability ratings. Like the alcoholics, the child molesters give significantly fewer extreme ratings and cling to middle ratings, a response characteristic which may be common to all character disorders.

31.   Cutter, F. "Rorschach Sex Responses and Overt Deviations." **Journal of Clinical Psychology,** 13(1): 83-86, January 1957.

The Rorschach Projective Test was administered to 25 sexual offenders under observation in a mental hospital, and the results were compared to the responses of 11 sexual offenders who openly admitted their behavior, and to 14 sexual offenders who continued to deny their behavior. All three groups contained a significant number of child molesters. Special attention was paid to whether sexual responses were given to Cards VI and VII since it is hypothesized that such responses are indicative of subjects with sexual deviation. No support for this hypothesis is found in this study, however; sexual responses to these cards is found to be more indicative of the severity of emotional disturbance than the overtness of the sexual deviation.

32.   Dingman, H.; Frisbie, L.; and Vanasek, F. "Erosion of Morale in Resocialization of Pedophiles." **Psychological Reports,** 23(3, Pt. 1): 792-794, December 1968.

An "erosion of morale" is documented in the semantic differential responses of 79 child molesters who were tested one year after their return to the community following a brief commitment to a mental hospital. Employment problems, family conflicts, alcohol use, and anxiety over the resurgence of sexual fantasies about children are believed to be contributing factors to their tendency to describe both the real and the ideal self in negative terms. It is predicted that sexual recidivism may increase as the self-image of the child molester becomes progressively negative, and as the ideal self standards deteriorate.

33.   Fisher, G. "Relationship Between Diagnosis of Neuropsychiatric Disorder, Sexual Deviation, and the Sex of the First Drawn Figure." **Perceptual and Motor Skills**, 9: 47-50, March 1959.

The first drawn figure in the Draw-A-Person Projective Test is thought to represent the individual's sexual identification and sex role preference. When the first drawn figures of a group of male and female neuropsychiatric patients are compared to those of a group of 32 incarcerated male sex offenders which includes 178 convicted child molesters, results show that the majority of each group tends to draw first a figure of his or her own gender. Since the results do not differ from those of normal subjects, the Draw-A-Person Projective Test is found to be an inadequate tool for differentiating between normal, neuropsychiatric, and sexually deviant groups.

34.   Fisher, G. "Psychological Needs of Heterosexual Pedophiles." **Diseases of the Nervous System**, 30(6): 419-421, June 1969.

When the results of the Edwards Personal Preference Schedule of 100 incarcerated child molesters were compared to test results of males in the general population, the child molesters score significantly higher on defiance, succorance and abasement, and lower in achievement, autonomy, change, heterosexual drive, and aggression. Compared to the scores of incarcerated non-sexual offenders, the child molesters score significantly higher on deference, abasement, endurance and intraception. Test results suggest a profile of the heterosexual child molester as a passive, subservient, insecure individual with strong dependency needs and a rigid, punitive conscience. He is unable to make effective decisions, has difficulties in expressing anger, and has conflicts over assertiveness and independence.

35.   Fisher, G. and Howell, L.M. "Psychological Needs of Homosexual Pedophiliacs." **Diseases of the Nervous System**, 31(9): 623-625, September 1970.

When the scores of the Edwards Personal Preference Schedule of 50 incarcerated homosexual child molesters are compared to those of males in the general population, the child molesters score significantly higher in abasement, intraception, and nurturance, and lower in achievement, order, autonomy and aggression. Compared to the scores of incarcerated heterosexual child molesters, the homosexual group scores lower in order and endurance. An unexpected finding is that the homosexual child molesters have a higher score in heterosexual drive than does the heterosexual group. Test results suggest a profile of the homosexual child molester as an unassertive, guilt-ridden individual who lacks achievement drive and inner direction, and who experiences low self-esteem.

36.   Freund, K.; Langevin, R.; Wescom, T.; and Zajac, Y. "Heterosexual Interest in Homosexual Males." **Archives of Sexual Behavior**, 4(5): 509-518, September 1975.

A sexual deviation questionnaire with a Feminine Gender Identity Scale (FGI), a Heterosexual Interest and Experience Scale (HetExp), and a Rated Homosexual Development Scale (Rh2D), was administered to groups of homosexuals with a preference for pubescent males, homosexual child molesters, and male homosexuals with a preference for adult sexual partners. No significant differences are found between the three groups on the HetExp and the Rh2D scales; a higher score on the FGI scale is found for those subjects who had the earliest onset of homosexuality and the least heterosexual interest and experience. All three groups show little heterosexual interest in general, and it is cautioned that if the goal of therapy with patients from these groups is to change sexual preference in the direction of heterosexuality, poor results should be anticipated.

37.   Frisbie, L.V.; Vanasek, F.J.; and Dingman, H.F. "The Self and the Ideal Self: Methodological Studies of Pedophiles." **Psychological Reports**, 20 (3, Pt. 1): 699-706, June 1976.
A semantic differential scale was created and administered to 223 child molesters who are on probation; the results are compared to the scores of 215 institutionalized child molesters. Each subject circled in black the adjectives that characterize "me as I am," and in red those that describe "me as I ought to be." Few apparent differences are found between the two groups; each is able to judge which of the adjectives implies the more socially desirable trait, but both groups are less certain in evaluating the desirability of traits for the ideal self. It is hypothesized that those subjects who report minimal differences between their real and ideal selves when describing basic personality components are less amenable to change and more likely to recidivate than those who perceive greater differences.

38.   Hammer, E.F. "Relationship Between Diagnosis of Psychosexual Pathology and the Sex of the First Drawn Figure." **Journal of Clinical Psychology**, 10(2): 168-170, April 1954.
It is hypothesized that the drawing of a person of the opposite sex first in a projective drawing test is indicative of psychosexual identification confusion. To test that, 84 incarcerated sexual offenders, 33 of whom are heterosexual child molesters, and 20 of whom are homosexual child molesters, were administered the House-Tree-Person Projective Test. The subjects were asked to draw a house, a tree, a person, and then a person of the sex opposite to the one first drawn. A female figure is drawn first by 12% of the heterosexual child molesters and by 25% of the homosexual child molesters. Since those figures do not differ significantly from the percentage of rapists in the sample who drew the female figure first, it is concluded that there is little support for the hypothesis that this tendency is indicative of psychosexual identification confusion.

39.   Hammer, E.F. "A Comparison of H-T-P's of Rapists and Pedophiles." **Journal of Projective Techniques**, 18(3): 346-354, September 1954.
The House-Tree-Person Projective Test is especially suited for formulating psychodynamic pictures of incarcerated subjects. A sample of 33 child

molesters and 31 rapists were asked to draw a house, a tree, a person, and then a person of the sex opposite to that first drawn; they were then asked how old the tree is, how old both persons are, and whether the tree is dead or alive. The child molesters tend to assign a much younger age to the tree than do the rapists. Since the assigned age represents the felt psychosexual age of the subject, assigning a young age to the tree reflects the psychosexual immaturity of that group. The child molesters also assign a greater age to the female figure than to the male figure, reflecting the greater status they tend to give to women, especially in light of their own immaturity. Since most males tend to draw a figure of a woman that represents a socially acceptable sexual object, the fact that child molesters tend to draw an older and maternal female figure may be indicative of unresolved Oedipal feelings.

40. Hammer, E.F. "A Comparison of the H-T-P's of Rapists and Pedophiles: The 'Dead' Tree as an Index of Psychopathology." **Journal of Clinical Psychology**, 11(1): 67-69, January 1955.

Occurrence of a "dead" tree in a subject's drawing on the House-Tree-Person Projective Test is thought to be indicative of serious psychopathology. 15% of the 33 heterosexual child molesters, 3% of the 20 homosexual child molesters, and 6% of the 31 rapists who were administered the House-Tree-Person Test drew a dead tree. This suggests that there is a progression of pathology from the rapist, to the heterosexual child molester, to the homosexual child molester. Therefore, an increasing distance from an appropriate sexual object is equated with an increase in serious psychopathology, so the homosexual child molesters, who deviate from the norm in both the age and the sex of the partner chosen, are likely to be the most seriously psychologically disturbed.

41. Hammer, E.F. and Glueck, B.C. "Psychodynamic Patterns in Sex Offenders." **Psychiatric Quarterly,** 31(2): 325-345, April 1957.

A battery of projective psychological tests, including the Rorschach, the Thematic Apperception Test (TAT), and the House-Tree-Person Test, was given to 200 incarcerated sexual offenders, including child molesters, incestuous males, rapists, and homosexuals. Test results show that all four groups have a pervasive fear of heterosexual contact, Oedipal concerns, and feelings of genital inadequacy. In addition, all four groups show a tendency for schizoid or schizophrenic pathology, a lack of ego strength, a reduced capacity for fantasy, and a lack of introspection.

42. Hammer, E.F. and Jacks, I. "A Study of Rorschach Flexor and Extensor Human Movement Responses." **Journal of Clinical Psychology**, 11(1): 63-67, January 1955.

Movement responses to the Rorschach Projective Test reveal characterologically rooted conceptions the subject has of his or her role in life. Extensor movements are associated with assertiveness; flexor movements with passivity, dependence, and compliance; and blocked movements with indecisiveness and doubt. The movement responses to Rorschach Card III are analyzed for 40 heterosexual child molesters, 22 homosexual child molesters, and one bisexual child molester; results are compared to the movement responses of 43 rapists. Both the heterosexual and the homosexual child molestors have very few extensor responses and a higher number of flexor responses. Compared to the rapists, the child molesters as a group are significantly more passive and dependent, and show marked conflicts over assertiveness and decisiveness.

43.   Jensen, D.E.; Prandoni, D.R.; and Abudabbeh, N.H. "Figure Drawings by Sex Offenders and a Random Sample of Offenders." **Perceptual and Motor Skills**, 32(1): 295-300, February 1971.
The purpose of this study is to test the relationship between the Draw-A-Person Projective Test and sexual pathology by judging the overall qualities of the drawings and by looking for specific indicators of pathology. The drawings of 53 sex offenders, including child molesters, however, do not differ significantly from those of a matched group of non-sexual offenders. The results suggest that the Draw-A-Person Projective Test is a poor indicator of sexual disturbance and that it cannot be used to differentiate sexual offenders from other types of offenders.

44.   Langevin, R.; Paitich, D.; Freeman, R.; Mann, K.; and Handy, L. "Personality Characteristics and Sexual Anomalies in Males." **Canadian Journal of Behavioral Science**, 10(3): 222-238, July 1978.
Hypotheses from the literature regarding the personality characteristics of sexually deviant males are tested with the administration of standardized psychometric tests to a group of 29 heterosexual child molesters, 22 homosexual child molesters, and 27 incestuous men; results are compared to test scores for a control group. The hypothesis from the literature that child molestation is associated with femininity is not supported by the testing; child molesters score below average on the MF (Masculinity-Femininity) scale of the MMPI and the I scale of the 16-PF, both of which measure femininity. Support is found for the hypothesis that child molesters are more likely to be shy and passive; elevations on the Si (Social Introversion) scale of the MMPI, and on the A, E, and H scales of the 16-PF are noted in the groups tested. The hypothesis that both heterosexual and homosexual child molesters are emotionally disturbed is supported by indications of psychopathology in their MMPI scores.

45.   McCreary, C.P. "Personality Differences Among Child Molesters." **Journal of Personality Assessment**, 39(6): 591-593, December 1975.
The MMPI scores of a group of 18 convicted child molesters who have no prior criminal record are compared to those of 15 child molesters who do have a prior criminal record. First offenders tend to have a lower Pd (Psychopathic Deviate) scale, as well as lower Hs (Hypochondriasis), Hy (Hysteria) and Sc (Schizophrenia) scales. Results show that first offenders are less impulsive, unconventional, and alienated, although slightly more depressed than recidivating child molesters. No causal relationship is discovered between the number of prior offenses on the criminal record and the severity of personality disturbance.

46.   Paitich, D.; Langevin, R.; Freeman, A.; Mann, K.; and Handy, L. "The Clarke SHQ: A Clinical Sex History Questionnaire for Males." **Archives of Sexual Behavior**, 6(5): 421-436, September 1977.

The 225-item, self-administered Clarke Sexual History Questionnaire for Males measures the frequency and type of erotic outlet. It is administered in combination with the MMPI, the Raven Standard Progressive Matrices, and the Clarke WAIS Vocabulary Test to a large sample of hospitalized sex offenders which includes 24 heterosexual child molesters and 20 homosexual child molesters; results are compared to two separate control groups of normal males. Test results show a continuity between exhibitionism and heterosexual child molestation; the former group exposes itself to mature females while the latter group exposes itself to pubescent and prepubescent females. Passivity is a characterological feature of all of the child molesters. It is concluded that the Clarke SHQ is a useful addition to a battery of psychological tests in that it is able to determine the direction of the sexually deviant behavior.

47.   Panton, J.H. "Personality Differences Appearing Between Rapists of Adults, Rapists of Children, and Non-Violent Sexual Molesters of Female Children." **Research Communications in Psychology, Psychiatry and Behavior**, 3(4): 385-393, 1978.

No significant differences on the MMPI are noted in the scores of 20 rapists of children and 30 rapists of adult women, but these two groups do differ significantly from a sample of 28 nonviolent child molesters. Both of the rapist groups present an MMPI profile of aggravated hostility, resentfulness, social isolation, impulsiveness, and self-centeredness. It is hypothesized that their sexually assaultive behavior is motivated more by aggression than by sexual gratification. The nonviolent child molesters have an MMPI profile of insecurity, inhibition, and fear of heterosexual failure. Their molesting behavior is presumed to be motivated by the desire to satisfy sexual needs at an immature level of psychosexual development.

48.   Panton, J.H. "MMPI Profile Configurations Associated with Incestuous and Non-Incestuous Child Molesting." **Psychological Reports**, 45(1): 335-338, 1979.

The MMPI profile configurations of 28 child molesters and 35 incestuous males are very similar; for both groups the Pd (Psychopathic Deviate) Scale is the most elevated, with the D (Depression), Hy (Hysteria), and Pt (Psychasthenia) Scales also elevated. The lowest scale for both groups is Ma (Hypomania). Both groups have moderate elevations on the L (Lie) scale, suggesting both are rigid in their attempts to adapt to changing social situations and show a tendency towards despondency and low morale. The only significant difference in the profiles of the two groups is that the child molesters have a lower Si (Social Introversion) Scale. The profile that emerges from the testing is that both child molesters and incestuous males tend to be self-alienated, anxious and inhibited, and both have pervasive feelings of inadequacy, insecurity, and are inflexible in their coping strategies. The child molesters are significantly more socially introverted, and have lower self-confidence, poorer self-esteem, and more sexual immaturity than the incestuous males.

49. Pascal, G.R. and Herzberg, F.I. "The Detection of Deviant Sexual Practice From Performance on the Rorschach Test." **Journal of Projective Techniques**, 16(3): 366-375, September 1952.

The reponses of 20 incarcerated child molesters to the Rorschach Projective Test are compared to those of a matched group of homosexuals, rapists, and incarcerated nonsexual offenders. No significant differences are found in the number of responses to the test; however, when each group was asked to sort through the ten cards and point out those that could represent male or female sex organs, a procedure referred to as "testing the limits of sex," differences between the groups do emerge.

50. Rada, R.T.; Laws, D.R.; and Kellner, R. "Plasma Testosterone Levels in the Rapist." **Psychosomatic Medicine**, 38(4): 257-268, July/August 1976.

The psychosocial and biological factors involved in sexual offenses are examined in this study that compares 52 incarcerated rapists of adult women with a control group of nonviolent child molesters. Each group completed a questionnaire on demographic data, a battery of psychological tests, and was measured for testosterone levels in the blood. Both groups show a similar rate of alcoholism, with 38% of the rapists and 42% of the child molesters rated as alcoholic, and both groups have average scores in the normal range of the Megaree Overcontrolled Hostility Scale. The rapists have significantly higher scores than the child molesters on the Buss-Durkee Hostility Inventory. The two groups do not differ significantly in their average testosterone level.

51. Segal, Z.V. and Marshall, W.L. "Heterosexual Social Skills in a Population of Rapists and Child Molesters." **Journal of Consulting and Clinical Psychology**, 53(1): 55-63, February 1985.

To test the hypothesis that sexual offenders have deficits in heterosexual skills, 20 child molesters and 20 rapists were asked to initiate and maintain a conversation with a female experimenter for as long as they felt comfortable and up to seven minutes. The subjects were then asked to verbalize what they were thinking and feeling during the conversation, and their statements were compared to those of a control group. Each group was then given a battery of psychological tests, including the Quick Test, the Social Interaction Self-Statement Test, the Survey of Heterosexual Interaction, the Social Avoidance and Distress Scale, and the Callner-Ross Assertiveness Scale, all of which measure social interaction skills. Results of the self-evaluation and the tests show that child molesters have significant social inadequacies and marked deficits in mature, heterosexually-oriented social skills.

52. Stricker, G. "Stimulus Properties of the Rorschach to a Sample of Pedophiles." **Journal of Projective Techniques and Personality Assessment**, 28(2): 241-244, June 1964.

Using a semantic differential scale, 61 child molesters were asked to rate ten Rorschach inkblots. They show a response tendency to give neutral or irrelevant ratings and guarded, minimally revealing responses. Many more positive evaluations of the cards are given than was expected; this tendency is more often seen in children than in adults, and is indicative of immaturity.

53. Stricker, G. "Stimulus Properties of the Blacky to a Sample of Pedophiles." **Journal of General Psychology,** 77(1): 35-39, July 1967.
　　The Blacky Pictures Test was given to 64 child molesters who rated each card on a series of semantic differential scales. Results show that the child molesters tend to give guarded, minimally revealing responses, and tend to overuse positive evaluating responses, much in the manner of small children.

54. Vanasek, F.J.; Frisbie, L.V.; and Dingman, H.F. "Patterns of Affective Responses in Two Groups of Pedophiles." **Psychological Reports,** 22(3): 659-668, April 1968.
　　A semantic differential scale was given to 143 child molesters who were on probation or parole and the results were compared to the responses of 215 incarcerated child molesters. The purpose of the testing is to develop a predictive scale to supplement clinical judgment in estimating the future successful community adjustment of convicted child molesters, but since there are no significant differences between the two groups in their responses, no predictive scale could be developed.

55. Wagner, E.E. "Hand Test Indicators of Overt Psychosexual Maladjustment in Neurotic Males." **Journal of Projective Techniques,** 27(3): 357-358, September 1963.
　　A group of neurotic patients with well defined patterns of sexual deviation that includes child molestation, give significantly more sexually implicit and explicit responses to the Hand Test than do a group of neurotic therapy patients who do not have a history of sexual deviation. Results would suggest that the Hand Test is a useful tool for identifying individuals with sexual deviations.

Phallometric Studies

Perhaps one of the most consistently accurate methods of determining the sexual preference and the strength of the sexual drive of child molesters is through the use of phallometric measures. In the studies cited, the erection responses of child molesters to such stimuli as movies, pictures, audiotapes, books, and their own fantasies are measured. Since the erection response is largely beyond the conscious control of the individual being tested, the phallometric measurement method is believed to be an especially useful laboratory tool for the assessment of child molesting tendencies.

56. Abel, G.G.; Blanchard, E.B.; and Barlow, D.H. "Measurement of Sexual Arousal in Sexual Paraphilias: The Effects of Stimulus Modality, Instructional Set, and Stimulus Content on the Objective." **Behavior Research and Therapy**, 19(1): 25-33, 1981.

The phallometric responses of 48 sexual deviants, 16 of whom are child molesters, are measured while the variables of stimulus modality, instructional set, and stimulus content are varied. Results show that the videotape method of presenting stimuli is superior for all sexual deviants, with the exception of the rapists and the child molesters, although the reasons for their exception are not known. As a stimulus, slides are adequate but are inflexible, free fantasy poses problems with content analysis, and the audiotape method shows some promise as a stimulus modality for all types of sexual deviants. Instructional set and stimulus content are found to be less important variables.

57. Avery-Clark, C.A. and Laws, D.R. "Differential Erection Response Patterns of Sexual Child Abusers to Stimuli Describing Activities with Children." **Behavior Therapy**, 15(1): 71-83, January 1984.

To test the hypothesis that phallometric measurements are effective in distinguishing between nonaggressive and violent child molesters, 31 convicted child molesters are grouped as either more dangerous or less dangerous according to raters who reviewed their criminal and hospital records, psychological data, and police and court reports. Each subject then listened to audiotaped descriptions of sexual activities with children which varied on both a sexual and an aggressive dimension while penile responses to the tape were measured. Using a formula in which the highest average maximum percent erection response generated by aggressive cues is divided by the average maximum percent erection response generated by the consensual sexual activity audiotape, a Dangerous Child Abuser Index (DCAI) was developed. With the DCAI it is shown that the most dangerous child molesters have an average score of 1.04, while the least dangerous child molesters have an average score of .54. Results of this study support the hypothesis, even though half of the subjects tested were able to exert some conscious control over their phallometric responses. It is not believed, however, that this faking response significantly altered the outcome of the study.

58. Freund, K. "A Laboratory Method for Diagnosing Predominance of Homo- or Hetero-Erotic Interest in the Male." **Behavior Research and Therapy**, 1:85-93, 1963.

By using phallometric response measurements to erotic pictures of male and female children and adolescents, the diagnosis and classification of groups of hospitalized heterosexual and homosexual child molesters, and of hospitalized heterosexual and homosexual neurotics can be confirmed or rejected. The phallometric measurement is shown to be effective in evaluating sexual preference and can be used to determine the diagnosis of the subject, especially if he denies a certain sexual preference despite objective information to the contrary.

59. Freund, K. "Diagnosing Homo- or Heterosexuality and Erotic Age-Preference by Means of a Psychophysiologic Test." **Behavior Research and Therapy**, 5(3): 209-228, August 1967.

The phallometric responses to pictures of adult males, and of female children, adolescents, and adults, are measured for groups of homosexual child molesters, heterosexual child molesters, homosexuals attracted to adolescents, homosexuals preferring adult partners, and a control group of normal males. Test results demonstrate that heterosexual child molesters respond the most to pictures of female children and homosexual child molesters to pictures of male children. Testing indicates that phallometric testing can confirm the stated or diagnosed sexual orientation of the subject.

60. Freund, K. "Erotic Preference in Pedophilia." **Behavior Research and Therapy**, 5(4): 339-348, November 1967.

Measuring phallometric responses to pictures of male and female children, adolescents, and adults is demonstrated to be an accurate measure of the erotic preference of heterosexual and homosexual child molesters.

61. Freund, K.; Chan, S.; and Coulthard, R. "Phallometric Diagnosis with 'Nonadmitters.'" **Behavior Research and Therapy**, 17(5): 451-457, December 1979.

The phallometric responses of a group of child molesters, some of whom continue to deny having molested a child, were recorded to stimuli of slides of adults, children, and neutral landscapes. This technique is recommended for confirming the diagnosis of pedophilia and for confronting "nonadmitters" with their denial.

62. Freund, K. and Langevin, R. "Bisexuality in Homosexual Pedophilia." **Archives of Sexual Behavior**, 5(5): 415-423, September 1976.

Using phallometric measures in response to pictures of nude women and children, the possibility of undetected bisexuality in a group of convicted homosexual child molesters was examined. The 9 men who showed or reported bisexual tendencies are found to be significantly more responsive to pictures of pubescent females when they are compared to 13 homosexual males. That latter, group, in turn, responds significantly less to pictures of adult females.

63. Freund, K.; Scher, H.; Chan, S.; and Ben-Aron, M. "Experimental Analysis of Pedophilia." **Behavior Research and Therapy**, 20(2): 105-112, 1982.

The first part of this study tests the hypothesis that a sizable portion of a sample of homosexual child molesters is actually bisexual by assessing their phallometric responses to movie clips of nude males and females, and by rating their responses to a 12-item "Admitter" scale. Support for this hypothesis is demonstrated. The second part of the study consists of the development of a "phallometric bisexuality index" to be used to assess the presence and degree of bisexuality in heterosexual and in homosexual child molesters.

64. Hinton, J.W.; O'Neill, M.J.; and Webster, S. "Psychophysiological Assessment of Sex Offenders in a Security Hospital." **Archives of Sexual Behavior,** 9(3): 205-216, 1980.

Child molesters, rapists, physical attackers of adult women, and normal males were exposed to slides of adult females in heterosexual activity; films of a variety of sexual behavior between adults, adults with children, and between children; and a film of a 12 year old girl being chased and then raped by two men. To each stimulus, the subjects gave a rating of the "felt sexual arousal level" on a scale of one to ten while penile diameter, penile surface blood volume, and heart rate were being measured. Many of the subjects adopted a number of defensive strategies in reporting their level of sexual arousal to the stimuli. Although few differences in the stated and the measured responses are noted between the various groups, the child molesters and the rapists show a significantly higher level of sexual arousal to the film depicting the rape of the 12 year old girl. It is theorized that it is this aspect of violence in the sexual situation that most clearly differentiates the sex offenders from other groups, although a significant number of the normal males also showed sexual arousal to the rape film.

65. Quinsey,V.L.; Steinman, C.M.; Bergerson, S.G.; and Holmes, T.F. "Penile Circumference, Skin Conductance, and Ranking Responses of Child Molesters and 'Normals' To Sexual and Nonsexual Visual Stimuli." **Behavior Therapy,** 6(2): 213-219, March 1975.

Twenty child molesters were asked to rank slides in order of their sexual attractiveness; phallometric and skin conductance measurements were then taken as the slides were viewed. Results are compared to those of control groups of nonsexual offenders and of normal males. Even though they rank adult female slides as more attractive, the child molesters have the greatest penile and skin conductance responses to slides of children. When the child molester group is divided according to heterosexual, homosexual, and bisexual preference, the physiological responses to slides are consistent with their stated sexual preference.

66. Quinsey, V.L. and Carrigan, W.F. "Penile Responses to Visual Stimuli: Instructional Control With and Without Auditory Sexual Fantasy Correlates." **Criminal Justice and Behavior,** 5(4): 333-341, December 1978.

Nine males recruited from the community watched a series of slides that depicted female adults or children in varying degrees of nudity, and slides of a neutral content while phallometric measures were recorded. In one sequence, sexually explicit fantasy material referring either to sex with adults or with children was played on a tape; in another sequence, no taped fantasy material was played while the subjects watched the slides. Subjects were given instructions either to fake a sexual interest in the slides depicting nude children, with a promise of $5 for their faking, or to just relax and watch the slides. Results of these variations show that 78% of the subjects are able to influence their penile responses according to instructions; the addition of the audiotape only marginally reduces the influence of instruction. Previous studies that conclude that samples of child molesters have difficulty in exerting voluntary control over their penile responses to visual stimuli are questioned.

67. Quinsey, V.L.; Chapin, T.C.; Carrigan, W.F. "Sexual Preferences Among Incestuous and Non-Incestuous Child Molesters." **Behavior Therapy,** 10(4): 562-565, September 1979.

The phallometric responses of 7 child molesters to slides of persons of varying ages and both sexes are compared to those of 9 incestuous males. Results show that the child molesters have less appropriate sexual age preferences than do the incestuous males, suggesting that they are more motivated by the general developmental immaturity of the child than by the child's specific age or by their relationship to the child.

General Clinical Approaches

The following studies use a variety of different techniques for the clinical assessment of samples of child molesters. Particular attention to demographic data can be found in many of the cited references, and some of them also suggest how the molester approaches the child and secures her or his cooperation.

68. Apfelberg, B.; Sugar, C.; and Pfeffer, A.Z. "A Psychiatric Study of 250 Sex Offenders." **American Journal of Psychiatry,** 100(7): 762-770, May 1944.

In comparison to other convicted sex offenders, the 75 child molesters in this sample of 250 hospitalized sex offenders tend to be slightly older, are more likely to be foreign-born, and to be diagnosed as schizoid because of their eccentricity, self-centeredness, and withdrawal. Each had made an attempt at adult sexual adjustment but had failed because of the persistence of infantile sexual attitudes and the breakdown of inhibitors by alcohol or senility.

69. Atwood, R.W. and Howell, R.J. "Pupillometric and Personality Test Score Differences of Female Aggressing Pedophiliacs and Normals." **Psychonomic Science,** 22(2): 115-116, January 1971.

Operating under the theory that the pupils of the eye dilate in response to positive and accepting feelings regarding the stimulus being looked at, while pupil constriction occurs when the viewer is experiencing negative and rejecting feelings about a stimulus, a pupillometric study was conducted with 10 nonviolent child molesters and 10 offenders incarcerated for nonsexual offenses. Slides of nude, adult females produce pupil constriction in 8 of the child molesters and pupil dilation in 9 of the controls; slides of nude female children produce pupil dilation in 9 of the molesters and pupil constriction in 5 of the controls. Because pupil constriction and dilation are involunatry responses to stimuli, the pupillometric measurement is thought to be a reliable diagnostic and evaluation tool.

70.	Bliss, E.L. and Larson, E.M. "Sexual Criminality and Hypnotizability."
Journal of Nervous and Mental Disease, 173(9): 522-526, September 1985.

A sample of 33 incarcerated sex offenders, 9 of whom are child molesters, completed a questionnaire regarding the circumstances of their offenses, a self-report questionnaire with 305 items characteristic of eleven major psychiatric syndromes, and the Stanford Hypnotic Susceptibility Scale; results were compared to those of a control group of 48 normal males. Histories of self-hypnosis experiences or dissociations are reported for 66% of the sample, including 7 of the child molesters who as a group also have very high scores on the susceptibility to hypnosis scale. More symptoms such as anxiety, multiple personalities, and phobias are reported for this group as are childhood histories of antisocial behavior and sexual abuse victimization. The possibility that that childhood history combined with self-hypnosis experiences may lead to sexual offenses is discussed.

71.	Brandon, S. "Management of Sexual Deviation." **British Medical Journal**, 3(5976): 149-151, July 19, 1975.

The various types of deviant sexual behavior a physician is likely to encounter are described. The child molester is described as a passive, non-violent individual who is very amenable to therapy.

72.	Cohen, M.L. and Kozol, H.L. "Evaluation for Parole at a Sex Offender Treatment Center." **Federal Probation,** 30(3): 50-55, September 1966.

The clinical picture of all sex offenders, including child molesters, is that their antisocial and asocial behaviors arise from deficits in their ego skills so that they are unable to tolerate frustration or to develop healthy interpersonal relationships. As a consequence, they tend to be selfish, cynical, unable to work in social groups or to engage in goal-directed behavior, and they have an infantile value system. Psychotherapy, therefore, must focus on moving the sex offender from a pattern of immaturity and self-centeredness towards greater social sensitivity, control, and freer emotional responsiveness.

73.	Cohen, M.L.; Seghorn, T.; and Calmas, W. "Sociometric Study of the Sex Offender." **Journal of Abnormal Psychology,** 74(2): 249-255, 1969.

To test the hypothesis that an analysis of the interpersonal social skills of sex offenders is a more sensitive measurement for forming clinical subgroups than a medico-legal analysis, 38 child molesters and 27 rapists were given a sociometric questionnaire. Results show that the rapists who were clinically assessed as having shown displaced aggression have the best social skills, followed by the regressed child molesters who were clinically assessed as having molested children in response to stress and feelings of inadequacy. The results demonstrate that the sociometric questionnaire is a sensitive measure for determining clinical sub-groups of sex offenders.

74.	(Comment). "Sexual Offenses Against Children." **British Medical Journal**, 1(5488): 626-627, March 12, 1966.

A general overview of the clinical dynamics of child molestation is presented. Some of the more common myths about the molester also are addressed.

75. Fong, R. "Sexual Abnormalities II: Dangerous Deviations." **Nursing Times**, 74(25): 1062-1063.

A general overview of pedophilia, incest, bestiality, and sadism is presented.

76. Groth, A.N.; Birnbaum, H.J.; and Gary, T.S. "A Study of the Child Molester: Myths and Realities." **Journal of the American Criminal Justice Association**, 41(1): 17-22, Winter/Spring 1978.

Data from the backgrounds and the clinical descriptions of 148 convicted child molesters are used to debunk some of the more prevalent myths about this behavior. Contrary to popular belief, the child molester is not typically a "dirty old man," nor is he mentally retarded, or a stranger to the child, a drug addict or alcoholic, or a homosexual. He is rarely psychotic and usually does not become more violent over time, although he is likely to repeat his child molesting behavior.

77. Groth, A.N. and Birnbaum, H.J. "Adult Sexual Orientation and Attraction to Underage Persons." **Archives of Sexual Behavior**, 7(3): 175-181, May 1978.

The psychosocial characteristcs of 175 convicted child molesters are presented. They can be classified as fixated in their sexual orientation towards children where there is a temporary or permanent arrestment of psychological maturation resulting from unresolved developmental issues, or regressed when there is a temporary or permanent appearance of immature behavior after more mature forms of expression have been attained. The fixated child molesters tend to be slightly older than the regressed molesters, are more likely to be strangers to the children they molest, and are more likely to use force or intimidation to secure the cooperation of the children. Boys are more likely to be the targets of fixated child molesters, perhaps because of the process of identification.

78. Groth, A.N. and Burgess, A.W. "Motivational Intent in the Sexual Assault of Children." **Criminal Justice and Behavior**, 4(3): 253-264, September 1977.

A typology of motivations and behaviors in cases of child molestation is derived from interviews with 137 incarcerated child molesters and 74 children who had been sexually molested. In the "sex pressure" types of molestations, enticement and entrapment are used to gain the cooperation of the child; sex appears to be in the service of the molester's dependency and affection needs, and the child is perceived as a love object. The child, in turn, experiences the pressure for secrecy that is attendant to this type of behavior as a psychological burden and will describe many fears surrounding disclosure. "Sex-force offenses" may include both sadistic and exploitative assaults in which threats and intimidation are used against the child who is perceived as an object of sexual relief. Sex in that type of behavior is in the service of power and the child is usually overwhelmed by the behavior and may later emotionally and socially withdraw from family and friends.

79. Henn, F.A.; Herjanic, M.; and Vanderpearl, R.H. "Forensic Psychiatry: Profiles of Two Types of Sex Offenders." **American Journal of Psychiatry,** 133(6): 694-696, June 1976.

The psychiatric profiles of 116 child molesters show that they are unlikely to have a prior criminal record for violent offenses. Compared to a sample of 69 rapists, the child molesters are less likely to have been diagnosed as character disordered, and more likely to have been diagnosed as sexually deviant without other disorders. Organic brain syndrome, mental retardation, and schizophrenia are diagnosed for 40% of the child molesters, and alcohol and/or drug addiction is frequently a secondary diagnosis.

80. Kerr, N. "Special Handling for Sex Offenders." **Perspectives in Psychiatric Care,** 10(4): 160-162, October/November 1972.

Statistics on the commitments of over a thousand sex offenders to a state diagnostic center reveal that 69% are child molesters. They range in age from 18 to 75 years, with a mean age of 30 years; approximately 25% have previous convictions for sexual offenses on their criminal records, and over 50% have criminal records for non-sexual offenses.

81. Kozol, H.L.; Cohen, M.I.; and Garofalo, R.F. "The Criminally Dangerous Sex Offender." **New England Journal of Medicine,** 275(2): 79-84, July 1966.

Sixty child molesters, 10 incestuous males, two statutory rapists, and 61 carnal abusers of children make up a sample of sex offenders who have been committed to a diagnostic and treatment center under Massachusetts' newly created "Sexually Dangerous Persons Act." Experiences with group and individual psychotherapy show that a sex offender who is diagnosed as psychotic harbors an extremely dangerous potential which is increased if he is also experiencing hallucinations. Also, a child molester who offers extreme protestations of shame, remorse, and self-hatred must be regarded as highly potentially dangerous and as having a very poor prognosis.

82. Myers, R.G. and Berah, F. "Some Features of Australian Exhibitionists Compared with Pedophiles." **Archives of Sexual Behavior,** 12(6): 541-547, December 1983.

A sample of 65 child molesters is compared to a sample of 45 exhibitionists to discover if there is a link between these two sexually deviant behaviors. The child molesters tend to be older, are more likely to have experienced the death of their fathers, are less likely to describe a positive relationship with their parents, are less likely to have a stable work history, and are more likely to be alcoholics than the exhibitionists. The data would lead to the conclusion that child molesters and exhibitionists constitute two clinically distinct groups of sexually deviant individuals.

83. Pascoe, H. "Deviant Sexual Behavior and the Sex Criminal." **Canadian Medical Association Journal**, 84(4): 206-211, January 28, 1961.

A psychiatric review of all types of sex offenders is presented. The child molester is often suffering from castration anxiety and has feelings of masculine inferiority. Isolated acts of molestation are not likely to have negative effects on children.

84. Peters, J.J. and Sadoff, R.L. "Clinical Observations on Child Molesters." **Medical Aspects of Human Sexuality**, 4(11): 20, 32, November 1970.

The typical child molester is a passive-aggressive personality with feelings of inadequacy and tends to regress under stress. Approximately half of all child molesters are either alcoholic or use alcohol to reduce their inhibitions about sexually approaching children.

85. Power, D. "Children in Danger." **Nursing Mirror**, 152(5): 38-41, January 1981.

A general overview of the etiology and treatment of child molestation is offered.

86. Sadoff, R.L. "Myths Regarding the Sex Criminal." **Medical Aspects of Human Sexuality**, 3(7): 64-74, July 1969.

It is theorized that not all sexual deviants become sexual offenders, that some non-sexual crimes are motivated by sexual conflicts, and that there are a variety of psychiatric conditions that go into producing any one of the sexual offenses. Case histories of child molesters are used to illustrate these theoretical speculations.

87. Sgroi, S.M. "Sexual Molestation of Children: The Last Frontier in Child Abuse." **Children Today**, 4(3): 18-21, May/June 1975.

A general clinical overview of the dynamics of child molestation and its effects on children is presented.

88. Sullivan, R.A.; Schaeffer, J.L.; and Goldstein, F.L. "Child Molestation." **American Family Physician**, 19(3): 127-132, March 1979.

A general review of the extent and dynamics of child molestation is offered.

89. Summit, R. and Kryso, J. "Sexual Abuse of Children: A Clinical Spectrum." **American Journal of Orthopsychiatry**, 48(2): 237-251, April 1978.

Several types of child molestation are proposed, including pedophilic incest in which an erotic interest in children is acted on both inside and outside the family, and child rape which is perpetrated by chronically antisocial individuals.

90. Swanson, D.W. "Adult Sexual Abuse of Children." **Diseases of the Nervous System**, 29(10): 677-683, October 1968.

A review of the cases of 25 convicted child molesters referred for psychiatric evaluation shows that they share few characteristics in common. They range in age from 18 to 67 years and come from a variety of economic, social class, and family backgrounds. Their psychological problems vary as well, with most of them evidencing some kind of character disorder, but others with psychosis, neurosis, mental retardation, and still others with no diagnosable psychological problems.

91.   Swanson, D.W. "Who Violates Children Sexually?" **Medical Aspects of Human Sexuality**, 5(2): 184-197, February 1971.
Four clinical categories of child molesters are proposed: the classic pedophile has an exclusive and consistent sexual interest in children; the inadequate sociopathic pedophile is not exclusively attracted to children but will use them for immediate sexual gratification; the brain damaged pedophile may be mentally retarded or senile; and the situational child molester is usually schizoid or neurotic and will molest children when under stress.

Biological Considerations

The possibility that child molesting behavior may be physiologically or genetically based is quite intriguing. Especially for those molesters whose behavior is chronic and resistant to conventional treatment and therapy techniques, this hypothesis may hold the key to understanding their behavior. Studies to date, however, have generated inconclusive results.

92.   Freund, K.; Heasman, G.; Racansky, I.G.; and Glancy, G. "Pedophilia and Heterosexuality vs. Homosexuality." **Journal of Sex and Marital Therapy**, 10(3): 193-200, Fall 1984.
A statistical analysis shows that there is a higher proportion of homosexuality within the child molesting population than there is in the general population, suggesting that the development of sexual preference among child molesters is etiologically different than it is for normal males. A possible physiological basis for child molestation is considered.

93.   Freund, K.; Heasman, G.A.; and Roper, V. "Results of the Main Studies on Sexual Offenses Against Children and Pubescents." **Canadian Journal of Criminology**, 24(4): 387-397, October 1982.
This review of the literature on child molestation and incest briefly considers the possibility that these sexual behaviors with children may be biologically based.

94.   Gaffney, G.R. and Berlin, F.S. "Is There A Hypothalmic-Pituitary-Gonadal Dysfunction in Pedophilia? A Pilot Study." **British Journal of Psychiatry**, 145: 657-660, December 1984.
An intravenous infusion of synthetic luteinizing hormone-releasing hormone was given to 7 child molesters, 5 non-pedophile paraphiliacs, and 5

normal controls. The child molesters respond to the infusion with a marked increase in luteinizing hormones, suggesting that a hypothalmic-pituitary-gonadal dysfunction may be the source of their sexual deviation.

95. Gaffney, G.R.; Luric, S.F.; and Berlin, F.S. "Is There Familial Transmission of Pedophilia?" **Journal of Nervous and Mental Disease,** 172(9): 546-548, September 1984.

This study seeks to investigate familial patterns of pedophilia by means of a blind family history comparison of 33 child molesters with that of 33 hospitalized depressives, and with 21 non-pedophile paraphiliacs. Demographic data show that the child molesters were older at the onset of their pedophilia than the paraphiliacs were at the onset of their sexual deviation, and were almost twice as likely to have been molested during their childhood. Pedophilia is found in the family histories of 5 of the child molesters and one of the paraphiliacs; none of the child molesters has a family history of paraphilia, but 4 of the paraphiliacs do. Depressives, in contrast, have a very low rate of paraphilia in their family histories, and no incidences of pedophilia. The data propose that sexual deviance in the generic sense is not familially transmitted, but that a specific syndrome, in this case pedophilia, may be. Although psychosocial factors cannot be eliminated, it is hypothesized that genetic factors may be responsible for pedophilia.

96. Rada, R.T.; Laws, D.R.; and Kellner, R. "Plasma Testosterone Levels in the Rapist." **Psychosomatic Medicine**, 38(4): 257-268, July/August 1976.

The psychosocial and biological factors involved in sex offenses are examined in this study that compares 52 incarcerated rapists of adult women with a control group of 12 nonviolent child molesters. Each subject completed a questionnaire regarding demographic data, a battery of psychological tests, and was measured for testosterone levels in the blood. The two groups do not differ significantly in their average plasma testosterone levels.

97. Regestein, Q.R. and Reich, P. "Pedophilia Occurring After Onset of Cognitive Impairment." **Journal of Nervous and Mental Disease**, 166(11): 794-798, November 1978.

Four cases of child molestation that had an onset after the subjects had suffered illnesses that had left them with mild cognitive impairments are presented. Two of the subjects had had an acute myocardial infarction, one had a brain tumor, and the other had vestibular neuronitis; all experienced cognitive impairment, lack of initiative, loss of control over emotions, lack of insight, and rigidity in defenses during their recuperation, and each molested a child during this period. It is hypothesized that when child molestation occurs in the absence of previous sexual perversion, a medical assessment of nervous system functioning is warranted.

Developmental Considerations

A social learning model of child molesting behavior is found with some degree of frequency in the literature. Most of the cited references suggest that child molesting behavior and/or motivations are learned within the context of the family; some also suggest that a certain constellation of social factors within the larger society may be conducive to the learning of this behavior as well. The role of sexual trauma in the childhoods of molesters is noted in many of the following studies, and the possibility that there is some kind of relationship between the experience of being a victim as a child, and a victimizer as an adult is examined.

98.   Gebhard, P.H. and Gagnon, J.H. "Male Sex Offenders Against Very Young Children." **American Journal of Psychiatry**, 121(6): 576-579, December 1964.
It is hypothesized that men who sexually molest young children under the age of five are operating under special handicaps when compared to other types of sex offenders. To test that assumption, 60 convicted child molesters who had victimized very young children are examined, and are compared to data on over a thousand other sex offenders. Some similarities in the two populations are discovered: about half of each group came from broken homes or had experienced the death of a parent at an early age; both were approximately at the same age at the onset of their sexual deviation; and neither group has a particularly high rate of physical handicaps or of speech defects. The men who had molested very young children did show some relevant differences from sex offenders in general: they have a significantly higher rate of early sexual experiences with adults and/or other children in their backgrounds; they are more likely to be religiously devout; they have more experience with anal and oral sex; they demonstrate more sexual polymorphy; they are less inclined to be married and experience significantly more marital problems if they are; and they tend to be less well educated than other sex offenders, and are more likely to be intellectually impaired. It is theorized that the sexual reversion to a young child is a function of the breakdown of control over sexual behavior that is the result of an intersection between a current psychosocial stress and a potential for the behavior that is rooted in a disordered childhood. Four categories of child molesters are proposed: the pedophile, the mental defective, the psychosexually underdeveloped personality, and the alcoholic.

99.   Goldstein, M.J. "Exposure to Erotic Stimuli and Sexual Deviance." **Journal of Social Issues,** 29(3): 197-219, 1973.
A clinical research instrument was created to assess the degree of exposure to pornography during preadolescence, adolescence, and adulthood, and the emotional and behavioral reactions to that exposure. A 276-question structured interview was also developed to collect information on demographics, sexual attitudes, and sexual history. Subjects include 20 heterosexual child molesters, 20 homosexual child molesters, 20 rapists, 37 homosexuals, and 52 regular users of pornography, who are compared to a control

group matched for age, education, and economic level. Both of the child molester groups and the rapists report less exposure to pornography and less recent exposure to it than do the other groups, but they also report a higher incidence of masturbation to erotic material when they were exposed to it. The homosexual child molesters report a home life in which nudity was not tolerated and sexual matters were not discussed; their sexual education came from male friends. The heterosexual child molesters also experienced little discussion about sex within their families; their sexual education tended to have come from male friends or from the clergy, and they are more likely to have had their first sexual experience with a prostitute than did the other groups. A summary of the data shows that sexual deviants report less average exposure to pornography than do the controls, suggesting that a reasonable amount of exposure to pornographic material, especially during adolescence, may be correlated with an adult pattern of acceptable heterosexual behavior.

100. Goldstein, M.J.; Kant, H.; Judd, L.; Rice, C.; and Green, R. "Experience with Pornography: Rapists, Pedophiles, Homosexuals, Transsexuals, and Controls." **Archives of Sexual Behavior**, 1(1): 1-15, February 1971.

　　Two groups of heterosexual and homosexual child molesters were asked to estimate the frequency of their exposure to pornography during their adolescence and adulthood, and the effects this exposure had on their behavior; results are compared to those of groups of homosexuals, transexuals, and controls. The homosexual child molesters have a lower incidence of having been exposed to pornography during their adolescence than did the other groups; whether this constitutes deliberate avoidance or stems from a greater interest in other types of sexual stimuli is not possible to determine. This group is also more likely to use pornography to masturbate than do the other groups. Heterosexual child molesters also report a low incidence of exposure to pornography and a high incidence of masturbation in response to it.

101. Groth, A.N. "Sexual Trauma in the Life Histories of Rapists and Child Molesters." **Victimology: An International Journal**, 4 (1):10-16, 1979.

　　A history of sexual trauma in the backgrounds of 178 incarcerated child molesters and 170 rapists was calculated and the rate of incidence was compared to a control group of 62 law enforcement officers who were matched for age and socioeconomic level. Sexual trauma is discovered in the childhoods of 31% of the child molesters; in most cases, that sexual trauma consisted of incidents of forcible sexual assault that occurred before the age of thirteen. This rate is significantly higher than that discovered in the childhoods of rapists and of the control group.

102. Hammer, E.F. "Symptoms of Sexual Deviation: Dynamics and Etiology." **Psychoanalytic Review**, 55(1): 5-27, Spring 1968.

　　One extensive case study of a 30 year old homosexual pedophile is presented to illustrate the psychoanalytic theory of the development of sexually deviant behavior. It is theorized that castration anxiety and Oedipal concerns are more intense for sexual offenders, and that their concrete orientation to reality with their lowered capacity for fantasy and sublimation are the result of early sexual experiences that probably occurred within the home.

103. Johnson, A.M. and Szurek, S.A. "Etiology of Antisocial Behavior in Delinquents and Psychopaths." **Journal of the American Medical Association,** 154(10): 814-817, March 1954.

Parental collusion may be both a major cause of, and a specific simulus for, such antisocial behavior in adolescents as firesetting, truancy, stealing, and sexual offenses. One case study of a sexually offending adolescent is presented in detail.

104. Marshall, W.L. and Christie, M.M. "Pedophilia and Aggression." **Criminal Justice and Behavior,** 8(2): 145-158, June 1981.

The police and court records of 41 incarcerated child molesters were examined to determine the extent of aggression in their molestation of children and to assess the possible etiological factors in that aggression. Records show that most are from the lower socioeconomic classes, have poor work histories, an average of an 8th grade education, and an average I.Q. of 93.3. Alcoholism is a feature of 66% of the sample; in fact, 54% of them were intoxicated at the time of the offense. The childhood experiences of 34 of the subjects are also examined. Most had experienced inconsistent and tense relationships with their parents; 32% had experienced frequent violent beatings, and the remainder describe a continuum of experiences that range from acceptable levels of discipline (18%), to excessively punitive discipline (15%), to parental rejection (9%). The rate of aggression found in this sample is thought to be a product of the disinhibiting effects of alcohol combined with this early history of childhood abuse and rejection.

105. McGuire, R.J.; Carlisle, J.M.; and Young, B.G. "Sexual Deviation as Conditioned Behavior." **Behavior Research and Therapy,** 2(3): 185-190, January 1960.

It is hypothesized that the learning of sexual deviancy is a gradual process over time that begins when the memory of a traumatic sexual experience is used as a fantasy during masturbation, thereby extinguishing other more appropriate stimuli for fantasy. The experiences of 45 sexual deviants, including 7 child molesters, are analyzed in support of this hypothesis.

106. Nedoma, K.; Mellan, J.; and Pondelickova, J. "Sexual Behavior and Its Development in Pedophilic Men." **Archives of Sexual Behavior,** 1(1): 267-272, February 1971.

An analysis of the sexual development of 100 incarcerated child molesters reveals that 40% never masturbated during adolescence, and 78% report occasional sexual intercourse with women their own age during their adulthood. An analysis of their crimes reveals that most of them approached children in socially appropriate manners and rarely used physical force or violence to accomplish the molestation; most of the child molesting acts involved fondling or masturbation. Only 36% of the child molesters viewed their own behavior as abnormal.

Age Factors

Child molesting behavior seems to be more prevalent within three distinct age categories: adolescence, mid-thirties, and senescence.   The child molesters who are in their middle thirties are most easily explained: they are a statistically more prevalent group, constituting a larger percentage of the general population; they may have a wider access to children; and they certainly are more likely to be the focus of law enforcement attention. The adolescent and the senescent molesters, then, become the subjects of the special attention of the following references.

107. Gigeroff, A.K.; Mohr, J.W.; and Turner, R.E. "Sex Offenders on Probation: Heterosexual Pedophiles." **Federal Probation**, 32(4): 17-21, December 1968.
A sample of child molesters on probation is examined. Three age groups appear to occur with some frequency among child molesters: the adolescent child molester tends to be psychosexually immature, has poor relationships with his peers, is dependent on his mother, and has a poor self-concept. The middle aged child molester is often regressive, alcoholic, experiences a great deal of stress, and has disruptive marriage problems. Lonely and isolated, the senescent child molester is unlikely to have a prior criminal record.

Adolescence

One of the critical developmental periods during which child molesting behavior may occur is during adolescence. The following studies examine the nature of the teenage child molester and the possible developmental factors that may have contributed to this behavior.

108. (Comment). "Adolescent Sex Offenders -- Vermont, 1984." **Journal of the American Medical Association,** 255(2): 181-182, January 10, 1986.
The Vermont Department of Health conducted a survey of caseworkers in the Department of Social and Rehabilitation Services and discovered that 161 adolescents had come to their attention for sexual offenses. Data on this sample show that 92% of the adolescents are males and have a mean age of fifteen years. Their victims range in age from two to sixty years, with a mean age of seven years. The adolescents in the sample sexually assaulted

people younger than themselves in 91% of the cases; and in 60% of all of the cases, penetration occurred. Some method of coercion was used in 81% of the cases. Data reveal that more than 25% of the adolescents received no psychotherapeutic treatment whatsoever, and that less than 12% of them received specialized treatment for sexual offenders.

109. Deisher, R.W.; Wenet, G.A.; Paperny, D.M.; Clark, T.F.; and Fehrenbach, P.A. "Adolescent Sexual Offense Behavior: the Role of the Physician." **Journal of Adolescent Health Care,** 2(4):279-286, June 1982.
This study of 83 adolescent male sex offenders discusses the role of the physician in diagnosing and treating the problem; 37% of the adolescents in this sample molested young children.

110. Fehrenbach, P.A.; Smith, W.; Monastersky, C.; and Deisher, R.W. "Adolescent Sexual Offenders: Offender and Offense Characteristics." **American Journal of Orthopsychiatry,** 56(2): 225-233, April 1986.
This statistical study of 297 adolescent male, and 8 adolescent female sexual offenders finds that 60% of the sample molested children under the age of twelve years. In nearly all of the cases of molestation, the child was related to or acquainted with the adolescent; and in many cases, the adolescent was babysitting for the child when the sexual contact occurred. Approximately 33% of the adolescents used physical force to secure the cooperation of the victim. The psychological profile of the adolescent sexual offender as it emerges from this study is that most experience significant social isolation and have academic and/or behavior problems in school. A childhood history of sexual abuse is discovered for 11% of the males and 38% of the females; physical abuse is found for 16% of the males, and both physical and sexual abuse during childhood is discovered for 7% of the males. The study concludes that adolescent sexual offenses should not be considered a normal part of adolescent development and are instead indicative of emotional and/or sexual problems that require immediate intervention.

111. Groth, A.N. "The Adolescent Sex Offender and His Prey." **International Journal of Offender Therapy and Comparative Criminology,** 21(3): 249-254, 1977.
The profile that emerges from a sample of 26 adolescent child molesters is that he tends to be an older adolescent, white, and that the child he molests is a white female. Drugs and/or alcohol play a minor role in the molestation which typically takes place in the child's home. Weapons are used in 33% of the molestations, and 75% of the sample of molesters had committed previous sexual assaults. As a group, the adolescent child molesters show significant emotional disturbance, identity conflicts, self-esteem problems, and developmental defects; all have a rigid, stereotypical image of masculinity.

112. Groth, A.N.; Hobson, W.F.; Lucey, K.P.; and St. Pierre, J. "Juvenile Sexual Offenders: Guidelines for Treatment." **International Journal of Offender Therapy and Comparative Criminology,** 25: 265-275, 1981.

The dynamics of juvenile sexual offenses are discussed and treatment strategies are presented.

113. Johnson, A.M. and Szurek, S.A. "Etiology of Antisocial Behavior in Delinquents and Psychopaths." **Journal of the American Medical Association,** 154(10): 814-817, March 1954.

Parental collusion may be both a major cause of, and a specific stimulus for, such antisocial behavior in adolescents as firesetting, truancy, stealing, and sexual offenses. One case study of a sexually offending adolescent is described in detail.

114. Kournay, R.F.C.; Martin, J.E.; and Armstrong, S.H. "Sexual Experimentation by Adolescents While Babysitting." **Adolescence,** 14(54): 283-288, Summer 1979.

Because of the responsibilities of single parents, the need for mothers to work, the rising divorce rate, and the high cost of day care, more children are being cared for by babysitters. A survey of 480 high school students shows that 92% have babysat on more than one occasion. Two cases are presented in detail to demonstrate the risk of adolescent babysitters engaging in sexually experimental behavior with young children in their care. It is questioned as to whether the potential benefits of such sexual experimentation outweigh the potential dangers -- experimentation in adolescence may lead to better adult sexual adjustment, however, premature sexual involvement also may result in displacement of unresolved neurotic problems, such as aggression, dependency and control, within the sexual arena.

115. Lewis, D.O.; Shankok, S.S.; and Pincus, J.H. "Juvenile Male Sexual Assaulters." **American Journal of Psychiatry,** 136(9): 1194-1196, 1979.

A sample of 17 juvenile sex assaulters is compared to a control group of 61 violent, nonsexual offenders. A battery of psychological tests, including the WISC, the Bender-Gestalt, and the Rorschach; a battery of educational tests, including the Woodcock Reading Mastery Tests, and the Key-Math Diagnostic Arithmetic Test; and electroencephalograph (EEG) test reveals that there is little difference between the two groups. Both show a history of general aggressive behavior that begins early in childhood and is exacerbated by exposure to a violent family life and by being victimized by physical abuse within the family. Both groups tend to show depressive and paranoic symptoms, illogical thought processes, and auditory, gustatory and/or olfactory hallucinations. Grossly abnormal EEG's are discovered for 23.5% of the sexual offenders, and 31.3% of the violent controls.

116. Litin, E.M.; Giffen, M.; and Johnson, A. "Parental Influence in Unusual Sexual Behavior in Children." **Psychoanalytic Quarterly,** 25: 37-55, 1956.

The possible collusive role of parents in the sexual acting out of children and adolescents is discussed.

117. Longo, R.E. "Sexual Learning and Experiences Among Adolescent Sex Offenders." **International Journal of Offender Therapy and Comparative Criminology,** 26: 235-241, 1982.

In a sample of 17 adolescent sexual offenders, most of whom had molested young children, a history of poor peer relations and a childhood history of physical abuse is commonly discovered.

118. Longo, R.E. and Groth, A.N. "Juvenile Sex Offenses in the Histories of Adult Rapists and Child Molesters." **International Journal of Offender Therapy and Comparative Criminology,** 27: 150-155, 1983.

This study of 231 adult rapists and child molesters shows that a history of sexual acting out, some of it with young children, is a common feature in adolescence. This suggests that sexual offenses when they do occur during adolescence should be viewed as a behavior that is part of a pattern that may develop into more serious sexual offenses at a later date.

119. Maclay, D.T. "Boys Who Commit Sexual Misdemeanors." **British Medical Journal,** 11(5167): 186-190, 1960.

The case histories of 29 adolescent male sexual offenders, 15 of whom had molested young children, are presented. A common theme found in all of these cases is the presence of an emotionally unsupportive family and the adolescent having developed an extremely insecure personality.

120. Reiss, A.J. "Sex Offenses: The Marginal Status of the Adolescent." **Law and Contemporary Problems,** 25(2): 309-333, Spring 1960.

The failure to accord adolescents a distinct status within society and the minimal institutionalization of norms for governing adolescent behavior have important implications for the definition and the sanctioning of adolescent sexual behavior. The difficulties in defining deviant adolescent sexual behavior are discussed, and the problems with the juvenile justice system's adjudication and disposition of these cases are examined.

121. Shoor, M; Speed, M.H.; and Bartlet, C. "Syndrome of the Adolescent Child Molester." **American Journal of Psychiatry,** 122(7): 783-789, January 1966.

Based on an anlysis of 80 adolescent child molesters, the following profile emerges: he is in his mid-adolescence; has an average I.Q. of 108 although his academic achievement is low; tends to be passive-aggressive with confusion over sex roles; and has no previous criminal record. He typically is a loner and prefers the company of younger children, and comes from a family in which his mother, with whom he identifies, is dominant and over-protective. Little concern about the sexually victimized child is demonstrated by either the adolescent or his family. Three cases are presented in detail to illustrate these dynamics.

122. Szurek, S.A. "Concerning the Sexual Disorders of Parents and Their Children." **Journal of Nervous and Mental Disease,** 120(5-6): 369-378, November/December 1954.

Two case studies are presented in detail to illustrate the theory that impulsive and/or antisocial sexual behavior in children is related to inappropriate attitudes and behaviors of their parents.

123. Waggoner, R.W. and Boyd, D.A. "Juvenile Aberrant Sexual Behavior." **American Journal of Orthopsychiatry,** 11(2): 275-291, April 1941.

Twenty-five cases of adolescents who have engaged in sexually deviant behavior are evaluated; 5 of those cases involve the sexual molestation of a young child. Several general types of adolescent sexual deviants are posited from a review of the psychological assessments of these adolescents. The Type I adolescent is emotionally infantile, and lacks personal independence and self-reliance; his parents are overprotective and have strong attachment needs. A family history of violence and rejection is a feature of the Type II adolescent who becomes antagonistic and confused in his handling of the larger world. The Type III adolescent experiences sexual problems because of characterological defects that include weak inhibitory mechanisms, and often intellectual or physical defects. The Type IV adolescent's sexual misbehavior is a product of a larger pattern of delinquent and antisocial behavior.

Senescent Child Molesters

Research demonstrates that the stereotype of the child molester as a "dirty old man" is much more myth than fact. The following references look at the senescent child molesters.

124. Henninger, J.M. "The Senile Sex Offender." **Mental Hygiene,** 23(3): 436-444, July 1939.

Sexual behavior directed against young children may be a feature of senility in males. Those men who do molest children may be sublimating their sexual drive by engaging in behavior designed to regain their lost youth. Five cases are presented in detail; methods of evaluation and problems with the disposition of these cases are also discussed.

125. Whiskin, F.E. "The Geriatric Sex Offender." **Medical Aspects of Human Sexuality,** 4(4): 125, 129, April 1970.

Two case histories of senescent men who sexually molested children are presented. It is hypothesized that the primary motivation in these types of acts is the need to recapture the sexual capacity of youth by an elderly male who feels lonely and may be experiencing regressive behavior.

Marital Relationship

The possibilities that the wives of child molesters may be aware of what their husbands are doing, and that they actually may play a collusive role in their husbands' child molesting behavior are considered in the following references.

126. Bastani, J.B. and Kentsmith, D.R. "Psychotherapy with Wives of Sexual Deviants." **American Journal of Psychotherapy,** 34(1): 20-25, January 1980.

Nine women who are married to sexually deviant men all express a fear of social condemnation because of their husbands' behavior. Believing that they had not sexually fulfilled their husbands, they blame themselves for their deviance. All of the women have poor self-concepts, and strong needs for reassurance and approval. Poor relationships with their mothers are noted, and in all of the cases, their fathers are described as detached or absent. All of the women married early, and although only two of the women were aware of their behavior, most of the rest suspected but said or did nothing. The ego defenses of denial, rationalization, intellectualization, isolation of effect, and undoing are commonly used by these women. All of them clearly identify with their husbands' aggression and the roots of their repressed hostility towards other women are found in their childhoods. Little empathy for their husbands' victims is noted. Five of the women are married to child molesters, and detailed case histories are given for two of them.

127. Hitchens, E.W. "Denial: An Identified Theme in Marital Relationships of Sex Offenders." **Perspectives in Psychiatric Care**, 10(4): 152-159, October/November 1972.

Wives of hospitalized sex offenders were asked to join their husbands in therapy. Denial emerges as a major theme in their marital relationships; as a defense it protects the wives from the perception of and confrontation with the unpleasant reality of their husbands' behavior. In addition, most of the women question their own sexual attractiveness and self-worth. Psychodrama and confrontation are used in therapy to address and resolve these issues.

Other Approaches

A variety of other approaches to the understanding of the child molester can be found in the literature. Using case studies, retrospective record reviews, and theory formation, these references attempt to broaden the knowledge about the motivations, feelings, and cognitions of the child molester.

128. Abel, G.G.; Becker, J.V.; and Cunningham-Rathner, J. "Complications, Consent, and Cognitions in Sex Between Children and Adults." **International Journal of Law and Psychiatry**, 7(1): 89-103, 1984.

An adult who has sex with a child develops a set of cognitive distortions that support this behavior. His unwillingness or inability to validate these beliefs by sharing them with other adults creates a situation in which these distorted cognitions are never checked against reality. This fact is underscored by interviews with 90 adult and adolescent child molesters, all of whom initially denied their sexual involvement with children. When these subjects were then assured of the confidentiality of any disclosures, their admission rate increased to 1%. When they were next asked to sort cards and indicate which kinds of described and depicted sexual acts were arousing to them, the rate of admission increased to 19%. The next step was a reinterview with the subjects that increased the rate of admission to 20%; and finally, the subjects were confronted with the laboratory assessment of the sources of their sexual arousal and that confrontation increased the rate of admission to 62%.

129. Bowman, K.M. "The Problem of the Sex Offender." **American Journal of Psychiatry**, 108(4): 250-257, October 1951.

Several types of sexual offenders, including child molesters, are discussed. The child molesters are described as passive, often impotent, men who feel inadequate around adult women. They turn to children as a source of vicarious pleasure and the role of the child as a seducer is also discussed.

130. Cassity, J. "Psychological Considerations of Pedophilia." **Psychoanalytic Review**, 14: 189-199, 1927.

Four cases of child molestation are reviewed in detail. It is theorized that there are two basic types of child molesters: those whose deviant sexual behavior developed as a result of a severe trauma during weaning, and those who have a distorted identification with the mother-figure.

131. Cavallin, H. "Dangerous Sexual Offenders." **Medical Aspects of Human Sexuality**, 6(6): 134-148, June 1972.

The literature is reviewed as to the dynamics of various types of dangerous sexual offenders, including violent child molesters.

132. Cliffe, M.J. and Parry, S.J. "Matching to Reinforcer Value: Human Concurrent Variable-Interval Performance." **Quarterly Journal of Experimental Psychology**, 32(4): 557-570, November 1980.

A 36 year old incarcerated child molester is asked to choose between pairs of sexual stimuli in a procedure with reinforcement arranged according to concurrent-interval, variable-interval schedules. The results support the use of this technique in the prediction of choice.

133. Conte, J.R. "Progress in Treating the Sexual Abuse of Children." **Social Work**, 29(3): 258-262, May/June 1984.

Data from published studies are presented to challenge the belief that child molesters and incestuous males constitute two distinct clinical categories. Another belief, that child molestation is only a mental health problem, is challenged as well. The economic, cultural, religious, and social factors that support it and prevent intervention must be recognized.

134. Conte, J.R. "Clinical Dimensions of Adult Sexual Abuse of Children." **Behavioral Sciences and the Law**, 3(4): 341-354, Autumn 1985.

Some of the more commonly held concepts among community mental health professionals who treat child molesters are challenged; these include the artificial and empirically unsupported distinction between a regressed and a fixated child molester, and between an incest offender and a pedophile. An alternative model for describing child molestation is offered. The model emphasizes the defense mechanism of denial so often used by the molester, cognitive distortions that support the denial and provide the motivation for the act, the process of sexual arousal to children, the sexual fantasies the molester has, his or her deficits in social skills, and the overlay of other social and/or psychological problems.

135. Curtis, J.M. "Factors in Sexual Abuse of Children." **Psychological Record,** 58(2): 591-597, April 1986.

Clinicians often use a hit-and-miss method in identifying cases of child molestation, and because of mandatory reporting laws, it is especially important that factors that the literature has identified as particularly conducive to molestation be identified. These factors should include: the family dynamics, particularly in cases of suspected incest; the presence of psychopathology and/or substance abuse in the alleged molester; a tendency for isolation, social ineptitude and withdrawal on the part of the molester or the family of the child; the personal history of the alleged perpetrator; and the psychosocial crises and stresses the alleged perpetrator may have been experiencing.

136. Finkelhor, D. and Araji, S. "Explanations of Pedophilia." **Journal of Sex Research,** 22(2): 145-161, May 1986.

The literature of pedophilia is reviewed and is integrated into a multiple factor theory. The four factors that are delineated as necessary for explaining acts of child molestation are: emotional congruence, or the fit between the adult's emotional needs and the child's characteristics; sexual arousal, or the development of a psychophysiological response to a child; blockage, or the constraints and restraints that interfere with the development of adult heterosexual relationships; and disinhibition, or the circumvention of ordinary controls.

137. Freund, K.; Seeley, H.R.; Marshall, W.E.; and Glinfort, E.K. "Sexual Offenders Needing Special Assessment and/or Therapy." **Canadian Journal of Criminology and Corrections,** 14(4): 345-365, October 1972.

A Sexual Deviation Questionnaire was developed to assist in the detection of true sexual deviation in a group of convicted sex offenders. It is found to be especially helpful in identifying those with pedophile tendencies.

138. Freund, K. "Diagnosis and Treatment of Forensically Significant Anomalous Erotic Preferences." **Canadian Journal of Criminology and Corrections,** 18(3): 181-189, July 1976.

Three abnormal erotic preferences, including pedophilia, are examined as to their characteristics, proper diagnosis, and prognosis.

139. Frisbie, L.V. "Charg-A-Crime: The Sex Offender's Equivocation." **Mental Hygiene,** 52(3): 462-466, July 1968.

When charged with a sex crime, the person often experiences some immediate rewards and delayed fringe benefits which may include the reduction or dismissal of the charges, creating a "charg-a-crime" reaction in which the person does the crime now and pays for it later. An analysis of the criminal charges against 887 adult male sex offenders, 425 of whom are child molesters, reflects the unpredictability of the legal system in cases of sexual offenses.

140. Frosch, J. and Bromberg, W. "The Sex Offender: A Psychiatric Study." **American Journal of Orthopsychiatry**, 9(4): 761-776, October 1939.

The 120 child molesters in a sample of 709 convicted sex offenders referred for psychiatric evaluation are most often diagnosed as sexual psychopaths. As a group, they tend to be of average intelligence, white, and practice a recognized religion; approximately half were under the influence of alcohol at the time of the molestation.

141. Gigeroff, A.K.; Mohr, J.W.; and Turner, R.E. "Sex Offenders on Probation: Heterosexual Pedophiles." **Federal Probation**, 32(4): 17-21, December 1968.

A sample of child molesters under probation supervision is examined. Chronic child molestation is rare, and the recidivism rate is between 7% and 13%. Recidivism can rise to 33% if the child molester has a previous conviction for child molestation on his criminal record, and to 50% if he also has a previous conviction for a non-sexual offense.

142. Gigeroff, A.K.; Mohr, J.W.; and Turner, R.E. "Sex Offenders on Probation: An Overview." **Federal Probation**, 33(2): 22-26, June 1969.

Guidelines for conducting the presentence investigation and for the probation supervision of a variety of convicted sex offenders, including child molesters, are presented.

143. Hartman, A.A. and Nicolay, R.C. "Sexually Deviant Behavior in Expectant Fathers." **Journal of Abnormal Psychology**, 71(3): 232-234, June 1966.

The purpose of this study is to investigate the antisocial behavior of expectant fathers. A total of 91 men whose wives were pregnant and who were arrested and referred for psychiatric evaluation were compared to a matched group of 91 arrested men whose wives were not pregnant. The expectant fathers are over two times more likely to have been arrested for sexual offenses that range from exhibitionism, to rape, to child molestation. It is theorized that sexual deprivation and/or the personal and economic stress that these men experience because of their wives pregnancies may create an immature, adjustive reaction that leads to sexually inappropriate and illegal behavior.

144. Heim, N. "Sexual Behavior of Castrated Sex Offenders." **Archives of Sexual Behavior**, 10(1): 11-19, February 1981.

Information from a questionnaire sent to 39 West German sex offenders who had volunteered for surgical castration and who had been released into the community after their surgery shows that their sexual responsiveness is more varied than expected. Six of the 19 child molesters in the sample still practice masturbation and/or coitus. A number of physiological and biochemical reasons for this unexpected finding are posited, and the practice of releasing castrated sex offenders six months after their surgery under the assumption that the hormonal loss is complete, is challenged.

145. Howell, L.M. "Clincial and Research Impressions Regarding Murder and Sexually Perverse Crimes." **Psychotherapy and Psychosomatics,** 21(1-6): 156-159, 1972/1973.

Child molesters referred for psychiatric evaluation after conviction demonstrate problems in the areas of assertiveness, decision-making, and self-esteem. As a group they tend to have strong dependency needs and rigid, punitive consciences.

146. Kurland, M.L. "Pedophilia Erotica." **Journal of Nervous and Mental Disease,** 131(1): 394-403, July 1960.

Three cases of child molesters are described in detail. All three men were unable to develop meaningful sexual relationships with adult women and it is hypothesized that fear of maternal separation may play an etiological role in this difficulty. When as adults they are faced with the biological necessity of responding to their sexual drives, they fail in mature, heterosexual expression and therefore substitute a prepubescent image of themselves which is projected onto the child they molest; that, in turn, allows them an outlet for their sexual energy while at the same time enabling them to retain their idealized and distorted images of themselves as small children. All of the men have episodes of depersonalization and of grandiosity, and all express unkind and even murderous feelings towards their siblings.

147. Kutchinsky, B. "The Effect of Easy Availibility of Pornography on the Incidence of Sex Crimes: The Danish Experience." **Journal of Social Issues,** 29(3): 163-181, 1973.

With the exception of rape, all sex crimes, especially voyeurism, verbal indecency, and child molestation, have shown a steady decrease since the 1976 liberalization of pornography laws in Denmark. In the case of child molestation, that that decrease is simply a product of a decrease in reporting is refuted; surveys of Danish citizens show a consistently strong negative reaction to this behavior and a consistently high reporting rate. It is theorized that child molestation as a crime has actually decreased and that the availability of pornography is a causal factor in that change.

148. Leppman, F. "Essential Difference Between Sex Offenders." **Journal of Criminal Law and Criminology,** 32(3): 366-380, June 1941.

A wide variety of sexual offenses are reviewed from a psychiatric perspective. Child molesters are described as psychosexually infantile individuals whose own sexual experiences as children may be the motivating factor in their deviance as adults. The role that schizophrenia, senility, and clouded consciousness may play in these offenses is also discussed.

149. Lindner, H. "Sexual Responsiveness to Perceptual Tests in a Group of Sexual Offenders." **Journal of Personality,** 21(3): 364-374, March 1953.

A sample of 67 incarcerated sex offenders, eight of whom are child molesters, was given two specially constructed tests of perception. To test the hypothesis that sexual offenders are more perceptually sensitized to sexual material, their responses to the tests are compared to those of a matched control group of incarcerated, non-sexual offenders. Results show that sexual offenders as a group more frequently and earlier attach sexual identification to the test drawings; and give more homosexual, aggressive, and authoritarian responses to test stimuli than do the controls.

150. Marshall, W.L. and Christie, M.M. "Pedophilia and Aggression." **Criminal Justice and Behavior,** 8(2): 145-158, June 1981.

The police and court records of 41 incarcerated child molesters are examined to determine the extent of aggression in their behavior and to assess the possible etiological factors in that aggression. Medical records and the interviews with the molested children show that 58% of the men used physical force in accomplishing the molestation and in each case the degree of force used was in excess of what was required to secure the cooperation of the child. The subjects in the sample frequently denied having used force and were often inclined to describe the molestation in nonviolent, even gentle, terms. This study casts serious doubts on assumptions in the professional literature that child molesters are essentially passive and nonviolent.

151. McCaghy, C.H. "Drinking and Deviance Disavowal: The Case of Child Molesters." **Social Problems,** 16(1): 43-49, Summer 1968.

Deviance disavowal is an attempt to sustain a definition of oneself as "normal" after one is regarded by others or is officially labeled as deviant. A total of 158 child molesters were interviewed to determine their deviance disavowal techniques. Alcohol intoxication is the rationalization offered by 44% of the molesters, and 18% of them completely deny having committed the act. Since part of maintaining a normal identity is to distinguish oneself from those lableled deviant, 109 molesters in the sample were asked to attribute motives to the other child molesters; those who deny that they themselves are molesters tend to attribute the most derogatory motives to others, while those who admit they are molesters attribute the least derogatory motives. When asked to suggest a legal disposition for other molesters, those who deny tend to suggest the most punitive dispositions for others, while those who admit suggest the least punitive dispositions.

152. Mohr, J.W. "The Pedophilias: Their Clinical, Social and Legal Implications." **Canadian Psychiatric Association Journal,** 7(5): 255-260, 1962.

The three aims of child molestation are the immature gratification of sexual impulses, the expression of deviant sexual tendencies, and the desire for genital union. Heterosexual child molesters tend to lack sexual maturation and are regressive under stress; homosexual child molesters tend to be more fixated and therefore are more repetitive in their behavior.

153. Mohr, J.W. "A Child Has Been Molested." **Medical Aspects of Human Sexuality**, 2(11): 43-51, November 1968.

Child molesters tend to be passive and inadequate and are rarely prone to violence. A variety of sources are cited to support this conclusion.

154. Quinsey, V.L. and Ambtman, R. "Variables Affecting Psychiatrists' and Teachers' Assessments of the Dangerousness of Mentally Ill Offenders." **Journal of Consulting and Clinical Psychology**, 47(2): 353-362, April 1979.

In order to determine whether psychiatrists' assessment of the dangerousness of mentally ill offenders meets the criteria for expert judgment, their evaluations of 30 cases, including 9 cases of child molesters, are compared to the evaluations of teachers who read the same cases. Each subject used a 9-point scale to predict future dangerousness; subjects also rated their confidence in their own assessments. Data show that neither group meets the criteria for expert judgment; in each group there is low interrater correlation and reliability. The psychiatrists do not use techniques of assessment that vary significantly from those used by the teachers. The expertise of psychiatrists in assessing and predicting dangerousness is questioned in this study.

155. Revitch, E. and Weiss, R.G. "The Pedophiliac Offender." **Diseases of the Nervous System**, 23(2): 73-78, February 1962.

Of the 1206 convicted sex offenders referred for psychiatric evaluation, 42% of them had molested a child under the age of twelve years. As a group, the child molesters are almost twice as old as the rapists in this sample, and may have engaged in the sexual behavior with children as a symptom of a general regression they had psychologically experienced. Based largely on interviews with the child molesters and a few of the children who were molested, it is concluded that many of the children acted seductively, therefore inducing the men to commit the offenses.

156. Rooth, G. "Exhibitionism, Sexual Violence and Paedophilia." **British Journal of Psychiatry**, 122(571): 705-710, June 1973.

A history of child molesting was examined in the backgrounds of 30 exhibitionists. Although only 17% of the sample reports having molested a child, and 6% having physically assaulted a child, it is hypothesized that exhibitionism and pedophilia are dominated by the same immature goals of genital display, inspection, and manipulation, and that exhibitionism, per se, is not a single clinical entity or syndrome.

157. Scott, E.M. "The Sexual Offender." **International Journal of Offender Therapy and Comparative Criminology**, 21(3): 255-263, 1977.

A review of all types of sexual offenders is offered. Two detailed cases of child molesters also are presented.

158. Segal, Z.V. and Marshall, W.L. "Heterosexual Social Skills in a Population of Rapists and Child Molesters." **Journal of Consulting and Clinical Psychology**, 53(1): 55-63, February 1985.

To test the hypothesis that sexual offenders have deficits in heterosexual skills, 20 convicted child molesters and 20 convicted rapists were asked to initiate and maintain a conversation with a female experimenter for as long as they felt comfortable and up to seven minutes. The subjects were then asked to verbalize what they were thinking and feeling during the conversation, and their statements were compared to those of a control group who also had participated in the same process. Each subject was also given a battery of psychological tests including the Quick Test, the Social Interaction Self-Statement Test, the Survey of Heterosexual Interaction, the Social Avoidance and Distress Scale, and the Callmer-Ross Assertiveness Scale, all of which measure social interaction skills. Results of the self evaluation and the psychological tests reveal that child molesters have the lowest scores on all measures, therefore demonstrating as a group a marked inadequacy in general social skills.

159. Socarides, C. "Meaning and Content of Pedophiliac Perversion." **Journal of the American Psychoanalytic Association,** 7(1): 84-94, 1959.

One case of child molestation is described in detail. It is theorized that the severe libidinal frustration experienced by the child molester combined with the overpowering aggression it produces leads to the act of child molestation which serves to prevent a psychotic episode.

160. Stokes, R.E. "A Research Approach to Sexual Offenses Involving Children." **Canadian Journal of Corrections,** 6(1): 87-94, January 1964.

This phenomenological study of 55 incarcerated child molesters concludes that heterosexual child molestation tends to occur accidentally and as a result of alcohol, while homosexual child molestation is more often carefully planned and is more likely to be repeated. Child molesters do not differ significantly in intelligence, social class, or educational level from the general public. Since child molestation seems to peak in three age levels -- adolescence, the late thirties, and the late fifties -- there may be three different types of pedophilia motivated by experimentation, by regression, and by the need to compensate for loneliness.

161. Swigert, V.L.; Farrell, R.A.; and Yoels, W.C. "Sexual Homicide: Social, Psychological and Legal Aspects." **Archives of Sexual Behavior,** 5(5): 391-401, September 1976.

A study of 444 homicides reveals that 5 of the murders were clearly sexually motivated, and that only one of those murders had a child as a victim. The data demonstrate that the popular perception that there is a high proportion of sex murders and that children are especially vulnerable to victimization is based more on myth than reality. The one case of the child who had been murdered by a homosexual child molester is explained in detail.

162. Toobert, S.; Bartelme, K.F.; and Jones, E.S. "Some Factors Related to Pedophilia." **International Journal of Social Psychiatry**, 4: 272-279, 1959.

This study of 120 incarcerated child molesters derives its conclusions from clinical observations of the subjects. Child molesters tend to be sexually dissatisfied, have strong religious interests, and inadequate interpersonal social skills. Most of them express strong feelings of guilt and remorse and are highly sensitive to the evaluations and judgments of others.

Recidivism

A special concern in the study of child molestation, and especially in the day to day supervision and treatment of child molesters, is the issue of recidivism. Predicting which child molesters will continue to pose a risk to children is an important goal shared by researchers and practitioners. The following references address that issue.

163. Dingman, H.; Frisbie, L.; and Vanasek, F. "Erosion of Morale in Resocialization of Pedophiles." **Psychological Reports,** 23(3, Pt. 1): 792-794, December 1968.

An "erosion of morale" is documented in the semantic differential responses of 79 child molesters who were tested one year after their return to the community following a brief commitment to a mental hospital. Employment problems, family conflicts, alcohol use, and anxiety over the resurgence of sexual fantasies about children are believed to be contributing factors to their tendency to describe both their real and their ideal self in negative terms. It is predicted that sexual recidivism may increase as the self-image becomes progressively negative, and as the ideal self standards deteriorate.

164. Fitch, J.H. "Men Convicted of Sexual Offenses Against Children: A Descriptive Follow-Up Study." **British Journal of Criminology**, 3(1): 18-37, July 1962.

The aim of this study is to determine what differences exist between heterosexual and homosexual child molesters, and between those convicted of subsequent sexual offenses and those who were not. No differences in intelligence or in age are found between the 77 heterosexual and the 62 homosexual child molesters, but the homosexual group has a higher rate of both prior and subsequent sexual offenses, thereby demonstrating a more persistent pattern of sexual delinquency. The homosexual child molesters are also more likely to be diagnosed as having a sociopathic character disorder, and as being fixated at an immature level of psychosexual development.

165. Freund, K. "Diagnosing Homo- or Heterosexuality and Erotic Age-Preference by Means of a Psychophysiologic Test." **Behavior Research and Therapy**, 5(3): 209-228, August 1967.

The phallometric responses to pictures of adult males, and to female children, adolescents, and adults were measured for a group of homosexual child molesters, heterosexual child molesters, homosexuals attracted to adolescents, homosexuals attracted to adults, and a control group of normal males. Test results indicate that both homosexual child molesters and homosexuals attracted to adolescents demonstrate a more persistent pattern of sexually deviant behavior and therefore are at the greatest risk for recidivating.

166. Frisbie, L. V.; Vanasek, F.J.; and Dingman, H.F. "The Self and the Ideal Self: Methodological Studies of Pedophiles." **Psychological Reports,** 20(3, Pt. 1): 699-706, June 1976.

A semantic differential scale was created and administered to 223 child molesters who are on probation; the results were compared to those of 215 institutionalized child molesters. Few apparent differences are found in the responses of these two groups. It is hypothesized, however, that those subjects who report minimal differences between their real and ideal selves when describing basic personality traits are less amenable to change and more likely to recidivate than those who perceive greater differences.

167. Gigeroff, A.K.; Mohr, J.W.; and Turner, R.E. "Sex Offenders on Probation: Heterosexual Pedophiles." **Federal Probation,** 32(4): 17-21, December 1968.

An analysis of a sample of child molesters on probation is presented. Only a small percentage of the sample are chronic child molesters and are truly dangerous in that they are likely to repeat their behavior; however, if the child molester has both a previous conviction for a sexual offense and for a nonsexual offense, the likelihood of his recidivating increases to approximately 50%.

168. Groth, A.N.; Longo, R.E.; and McFadin, J.B. "Undetected Recidivism Among Rapists and Child Molesters." **Crime and Delinquency,** 28(3): 449-458, July 1982.

The recidivism rate of a group of 54 incarcerated child molesters is determined through the use of a five-item questionnaire; their answers are compared to the data contained in their individual presentence investigation reports. The analysis shows that child molesters get away with two to five times as many offenses against children as resulted in apprehension, showing that contrary to popular perception, child molesters are serious recidivists. Because the child molesters also are inclined to minimize and misinterpret their deviant behavior, it is assumed that the actual rate of undetected recidivism may be much higher than what this study has uncovered.

169. Marshall, W.L. and McKnight, R.D. "An Integrated Treatment Program for Sexual Offenders." **Canadian Psychiatric Association Journal,** 20(2): 133-138, March 1975.

Three incarcerated child molesters were treated by pairing electrical shocks with slides of children and then terminating the shocks with slides of adults, with training in social skills, and by exposure to social interaction with staff on the ward and in the occupational therapy program. One subject was released and molested another child eighteen months later; one was released and has not recidivated after eight months; and the third is still incarcerated.

170. Peters, J.J.; Pedigo, J.M.; Steg, J.; and McKenna, J.J. "Group Psychotherapy of the Sex Offender." **Federal Probation,** 32(3): 41-45, September 1968.

The successful adjustment to community life of a sample of 92 sexual offenders, including child molesters, who had received intensive group psychotherapy was compared to a matched sample of sexual offenders who had received no therapy. The recidivism rate of the first group is significantly lower than that of the control group. The process of group therapy and the difficulties in working with this type of patient are also discussed.

171. Quinsey, V.L. and Ambtman, R. "Variables Affecting Psychiatrists' and Teachers' Assessments of the Dangerousness of Mentally Ill Offenders." **Journal of Consulting and Clinical Psychology,** 47(2): 353-362, April 1979.

In order to determine whether psychiatrists' assessment of the dangerousness of mentally ill offenders meets the criteria for expert judgment, their evaluations of 30 cases, including 9 cases of child molesters, are compared to the evaluations of teachers who read the same cases. Each subject used a 9-point scale to rate the personal injury inflicted in each case, and a 9-point scale to predict the future dangerousness of the offender. Results show that psychiatrists do not use techniques of assessment that differ significantly from those used by the teachers; their expertise in assessing and predicting dangerousness is questioned in this study.

172. Romero, J.J. and Williams, L.M. "Recidivism Among Convicted Sex Offenders: A Ten Year Followup Study." **Federal Probation,** 49(1): 58-64, March 1985.

A ten year followup discovers a recidivism rate of 6.2% for 39 convicted child molesters.

173. Vanasek, F.J.; Frisbie, L.V.; and Dingman, H.F. "Patterns of Affective Responses in Two Groups of Pedophiles." **Psychological Reports,** 22(3): 659-668, April 1968.

A semantic differential scale was given to 143 child molesters who were on probation or parole and the results were compared to the responses of 215 incarcerated child molesters. The purpose of the testing is to develop a predictive scale to supplement clinical judgment in estimating the future successful community adjustment of convicted child molesters, but since there are no significant differences between the two groups in their responses, no predictive scale could be developed.

Female Child Molesters

Studies on child molesters consistently have demonstrated that the molester is most likely to be a male; demographic studies, in fact, show that a male is the molester in anywhere from 95% to 100% of the cases examined. Although statistically rare, the female child molester has not been overlooked in the literature. The following references, each with small samples of female molesters, discuss the nature and dynamics of this apparently unusual type of child molesting.

174. Fehrenbach, P.A.; Smith, W.; Monastersky, C.; and Deisher, R.W. "Adolescent Sexual Offenders: Offender and Offense Characteristics." **American Journal of Orthopsychiatry,** 56(2): 225-233, April 1986.
　　Eight adolescent females are part of a sample of 305 adolescent sexual offenders analyzed in this study. All eight of the girls were under treatment for having engaged in indecent liberties with children age six or under. The molestation of the young children occurred during babysitting for 63% of the girls. All of the girls in the sample experience significant social isolation and have problems either academically or behaviorally in school. A childhood history of sexual abuse is discovered for 38% of the girls.

175. Freund, K.; Heasman, G.; Racansky, I.G.; and Glancy, G. "Pedophilia and Heterosexuality vs. Homosexuality." **Journal of Sex and Marital Therapy,** 10(3): 193-200, Fall 1984.
　　It is theorized that there may be a physiological basis to pedophilia because it is such a rare sexual deviation among women.

176. Petrovich, M. and Templer, D.I. "Heterosexual Molestation of Children Who Later Became Rapists." **Psychological Reports,** 54(3): 810, June 1984.
　　A childhood history of sexual molestation by a female is found in the backgrounds of 59% of the 83 incarcerated adult male rapists in this study. Their ages at the time of the molestation ranged from four to sixteen years; most had experienced sexual intercourse on repeated occasions with an older female who was not related to them. Speculations as to what kind of an impact these childhood experiences may have had on their adult sexually aggressive behavior with women are presented.

177. Sarrell, P.M. and Masters, W.H. "Sexual Molestation of Men by Women." **Archives of Sexual Behavior,** 11(2): 117-131, 1982.
　　There is a widespread belief that it would be impossible for a male to achieve or maintain an erection when threatened or sexually attacked by a female, but there is evidence presented in this study that both men and boys have responded sexually to assaults and abuses perpetrated by women,

even though their emotional states were overwhelmingly negative at the time. Eleven cases are presented in detail, four of which involve the sexual abuse of young boys by women. A post-assault syndrome, not distinctly different from the rape trauma syndrome described for female rape victims and which includes symptoms of depression, guilt, shame, anxiety and post-assault sexual dysfunction is documented.

CHAPTER 5:
HOMOSEXUAL CHILD MOLESTATION

As some of the cited historical references have demonstrated, the notion that homosexuals in general pose a risk to children is deeply rooted within culture. Most studies on homosexuality and on sexual preference in general would debunk that notion, but the belief seems to persist and is all too often easily mobilized by reported cases of homosexual child molestation that seem to give it credibility and substance.

Perhaps because that very belief is so persistent it has become a stimulus to research. Homosexual child molesters are the subjects of considerable interest in the literature, and the "double deviance" implied by the act has honed a keen attention to the nature and dynamics of this type of child molestation.

Clinical Descriptions

The following studies use a variety of techniques to assess the clinical dimension of homosexual child molestation. Special attention is paid in many of them to the differences in dynamics between the homosexual and the heterosexual child molester.

178. Fischer, G. and Howell, L.M. "Psychological Needs of Homosexual Pedophiliacs." **Diseases of the Nervous System,** 31(9): 623-625, September 1970.
When the results of the Edwards Personal Preference Schedule of 50 incarcerated homosexual child molesters were compared to those of heterosexual males in the general population, the child molesters score significantly higher in intraception and abasement, and lower on achievement, order, autonomy, and aggression. Compared to the scores of incarcerated heterosexual child molesters, they score lower in order and endurance. An unexpected finding is that the homosexual child molesters score higher in heterosexual

drive than do the heterosexual child molesters. Test results develop a profile of a homosexual child molester as an unassertive, guilt-ridden individual who lacks achievement drive and inner direction, and who experiences low self-esteem.

179. Fitch, J.H. "Men Convicted of Sexual Offenses Against Children: A Descriptive Followup Study." **British Journal of Criminology**, 3(1): 18-37, July 1962.

No differences in intelligence or age are found in this comparison of a group of 62 homosexual child molesters with a group of 77 heterosexual child molesters, but the homosexual child molesters are more likely to have been diagnosed as sociopathic and to have demonstrated more fixation at an immature level of psychosexual development.

180. Foxe, A.N. "Psychoanalysis of a Sodomist." **American Journal of Orthopsychiatry**, 11(1): 133-142, January 1941.

The successful psychoanalysis of an incarcerated homosexual child molester is described. The 37 year old man was convicted of sodomy with two boys in what is described as an attempt to act out his own lost boyhood. He had been molested himself at the age of eight by an older male, and had a variety of homosexual experiences throughout his adolescence.

181. Freund, K. "A Laboratory Method for Diagnosing Predominance of Homo- or Hetero-Erotic Interest in the Male." **Behavior Research and Therapy**, 1: 85-93, 1963.

By using phallometric response measurements to erotic pictures of male and female children and adolescents, the diagnosis and classification of groups of hospitalized homosexual and heterosexual child molesters are confirmed or rejected. The phallometric measure is shown to be effective in evaluating the sexual preference of subjects and can be used to determine the diagnosis when a subject denies having a certain sexual preference despite objective information to the contrary.

182. Freund, K. "Diagnosing Homo- or Heterosexuality and Erotic Age-Preference by Means of a Psychophysiologic Test." **Behavior Research and Therapy**, 5(3): 209-228, August 1967.

The phallometric responses of a large group of incarcerated sexual offenders, which includes homosexual child molesters, to pictures of adult males and of female adults, adolescent and children, are compared to a group of normal males. Testing indicates that both homosexual child molesters and homosexuals attracted to adolescents show a more persistent pattern of sexual deviance; therefore these groups have a higher probability of recidivism.

183. Freund, K. "Erotic Preference in Pedophilia." **Behavior Research and Therapy**, 5(4): 339-348, November 1967.

The erotic preferences of homosexual child molesters can be determined through the use of phallometric measures.

184. Freund, K.; Langevin, R.; Wescom, T.; and Zajac, Y. "Heterosexual Interest in Homosexual Males." **Archives of Sexual Behavior,** 4(5): 509-518, September 1975.

The homosexual child molesters in this sample of incarcerated sexual offenders have a social history with the least heterosexual interest and experiences. It is cautioned that if the goal of therapy with homosexual child molesters is to change their sexual preference in the direction of heterosexuality, poor results should be anticipated.

185. Freund, K. and Langevin. "Bisexuality in Homosexual Pedophilia." **Archives of Sexual Behavior**, 5(5): 415-423, September 1976.

Using phallometric measure in response to pictures of nude women and children, the possibility of undetected bisexuality in a group of convicted homosexual child molesters is examined.

186. Freund, K.; Scher, H.; Chan, S.; and Ben-Aron, M. "Experimental Analysis of Pedophilia." **Behavior Research and Therapy**, 20(2): 105-112, 1982.

The first part of this study tests the hypothesis that a sizable portion of a sample of homosexual child molesters is actually bisexual by assessing their phallometric responses to movie clips of nude males and females, and by rating their responses to a 12-item "Admitter" scale. Support for this hypothesis is demonstrated. The second part of the study consists of the development of a "phallometric bisexuality index" to be used to assess the presence and degree of bisexuality in homosexual child molesters.

187. Glueck, B.C. "Psychodynamic Patterns in the Homosexual Sex Offender." **American Journal of Psychiatry,** 112(7): 584-590, January 1956.

A battery of psychological tests was given to a group of 30 homosexual child molesters and the diagnostic portrait that emerges from the testing is compared to that of 30 rapists, and of 50 nonsexual offenders. The homosexual child molesters are less likely to be character disordered than the other offenders, and more likely to have been diagnosed as schizophrenic. Post-test interviews with the homosexual child molesters reveal that they have a pervasive fear of intimacy with adult females, and that the source of that fear may lie in the restrictive and punitive attitudes and behaviors of their parents. Chronic childhood anxiety that manifested itself in nightmares, enuresis, fears, and marked shyness is found in the backgrounds of 94% of the homosexual child molesters; it is theorized that that anxiety creates a nonintrospective orientation towards the environment during adulthood. All of the homosexual child molesters show a reduced capacity for fantasy release or other sublimatory behavior. Moderate to severe guilt feelings are documented for 79% of them; in most, the superego is so rigid and inflexible that it breaks down under stress.

188. Goldstein, M.J. "Exposure to Erotic Stimuli and Sexual Deviance." **Journal of Social Issues**, 29(3): 1970219, 1973.

A clinical research instrument was created to assess the degree of exposure to pornography during preadolescence, adolescence and adulthood, and the emotional and behavioral reactions to that exposure, and was administered to 20 homosexual child molesters who were part of a larger group of sexually deviant males. The homosexual child molesters report little exposure to pornography at all stages of their lives, but a higher incidence of masturbation to the material when they did see it. They also describe a homelife in which nudity was not tolerated and sexual matters were not discussed; their sexual education tended to have come from male peers. It is hypothesized that a reasonable amount of exposure to pornography, especially during adolescence, may be correlated with an adult pattern of acceptable heterosexual behavior.

189. Groth, A.N. and Burgess, A.W. "Male Rape: Offenders and Victims." **American Journal of Psychiatry,** 137(7): 806-810, July 1980.

Sixteen males who had sexually assaulted other males range in age from 12 to 41 years; their victims ranged in age from 10 to 30 years. These offenses are found to have been variously motivated by needs for conquest and control, for revenge, for degradation, for status, or by unresolved and conflictual sexual interests.

190. Hammer, E.F. "A Comparison of H-T-P's of Rapists and Pedophiles: The 'Dead' Tree as an Index of Psychopathology." **Journal of Clinical Psychology,** 11(1): 67-69, January 1955.

It is believed that a "dead tree" in a subject's drawing on the House-Tree-Person Projective Test is indicative of serious psychopathology. In a sample of sexual offenders, the homosexual child molesters are most inclined to give a dead tree response. The results suggest that there is a progression in the seriousness of psychopathology from the rapist, to the heterosexual child molester, to the homosexual child molester. Therefore, an increasing distance from an appropriate sexual object is equated with an increase in serious psychopathology, so that the homosexual child molester, who deviates from the norm in both the age and the sex of the partner chosen, is likely to be the most emotionally disturbed of the sex offenders.

191. Hammer, E.F. and Jacks, I. "A Study of Rorschach Flexor and Extensor Human Movement Responses." **Journal of Clinical Psychiatry,** 11(1): 63-67, January 1955.

The movement responses to the Rorschach Projective Tests are assessed for a group of 22 homosexual child molesters; results are compared to the responses of 40 heterosexual child molesters, one bisexual child molester, and 43 rapists. Both the homosexual and the heterosexual child molesters exhibit very few extensor responses which are thought to be associated with self-assertiveness; the two groups have more flexor responses which are thought to be associated with passivity, dependence, and compliance. Compared to rapists, then, both homosexual and heterosexual child molesters are significantly less assertive and more passive and dependent.

192. Langevin, R.; Paitich, D.; Freeman, R.; Mann, K.; and Handy, L. "Personality Characteristics and Sexual Anomalies in Males." **Canadian Journal of Behavioral Science**, 10(3): 222-238, July 1978.

Hypotheses from the literature regarding the personality characteristics of sexually deviant males are tested with the administration of a battery of psychological tests to 22 homosexual child molesters, 29 heterosexual child molesters, and 27 incestuous males; results are compared to test scores for a group of normal males. No evidence exists that homosexual child molesters are more feminine, but there is evidence that they are more shy and passive. Emotional disturbance as measured by the MMPI is also found for homosexual child molesters.

193. Sandfort, T.G. "Sex in Pedophiliac Relationships: An Empirical Investigation Among a Nonrepresentative Group of Boys." **Journal of Sex Research**, 20(2): 123-142, May 1984.

Twenty-five boys who have on-going, mutually agreed upon sexual relationships with adult males who are members of a Pedophile Workgroup in the Netherlands, participated in a structured interview which utilizes a Self-Confrontation Method that determines what is important for the person at a certain moment in his life and gives insight into the meaning of these events and feelings. All of the boys indicate a positive reaction to their sexual relationship with the pedophile and all believe that the relationship has a beneficial impact on their well-being. Although concerns about being discovered and punished did surface in the interviews, all of the boys stated that the pedophiles' attention to them, their respect for their feelings, and their friendship far outweighed the disadvantages of having such a relationship.

194. Swigert, V.L.; Farrell, R.A.; and Yoels, W.C. "Sexual Homicide: Social, Psychological and Legal Aspects." **Archives of Sexual Behavior**, 5(5): 391-401, September 1976.

A review of 444 homicides reveals that, contrary to popular perception, few are sexually motivated and children are not at a great risk for victimization. The case of one murder in which a child was killed by a homosexual child molester is presented in detail.

195. Tindall, R.H. "The Male Adolescent Involved with a Pederast Becomes an Adult." **Journal of Homosexuality**, 3(4): 373-387, Summer 1978.

This study looks at 9 adult males, each of whom had had a longterm sexual relationship with an older man when they were adolescents. As adults, none appears to have been emotionally traumatized by this kind of sexual relationship, and although a few of the men admit to homosexual fantasies and to some homosexual behavior as adults, none identifies himself as a homosexual. It is theorized that the lack of trauma and deleterious effects may be due to the fact that these had been consenting, non-coercive sexual relationships with men who were described as "fatherly" and with whom the adolescents had developed close friendships.

Treatment

The treatment of homosexual child molesters may involve one or both
of the following directions: changing the behavior so that children are no
longer a source of sexual arousal; or changing the behavior so that homosexuality is no longer the sexual preference. Certainly there has been little resistance in accepting the first goal as preferable; the second goal, however,
raises some interesting ethical questions that are debated in some of the following references.

196. Davison, G.C. and Wilson, C.T. "Goals and Strategies in Behavioral
Treatment of Homosexual Pedophilia: Comments on a Case Study." **Journal
of Abnormal Psychology**, 83(2): 196-198, April 1974.
      The decision in the Kohlenberg study (see reference number 199) to
work in therapy towards the homosexual, rather than the heterosexual, adjustment of a homosexual child molester is supported.

197. Foxe, A.N. "Psychoanalysis of a Sodomist." **American Journal of
Orthopsychiatry**, 11(1): 133-142, January 1941.
      The successful psychoanalysis of a 37 year old incarcerated homosexual child molester is described.

198. Garfield, S.L. "Values: An Issue in Psychotherapy -- Comments on
a Case Study." **Journal of Abnormal Psychology,** 83(2): 202-203, April
1974.
      The ethical dimensions of the decision presented in the Kohlenberg
study (see reference number **199**) to redirect the sexual behavior of a homosexual child molester towards adult males, are discussed.

199. Kohlenberg, R.J. "Treatment of a Homosexual Pedophiliac Using In
Vivo Desensitization: A Case Study." **Journal of Abnormal Psychology**,
83(2): 192-195, April 1974.
      This controversial case study involves the treatment of a homosexual
child molester by pairing electrical shocks with pictures of nude boys; once
arousal to this stimulus was reduced, the subject was encouraged to actually
engage in a graded sequence of sexual interactions with an adult male. This
"in vivo" desensitization process produced a significant change in the subject's behavior; he became sexually aroused to adult males and significantly
reduced his sexual behavior with and sexual fantasies about young boys.

200. Laws. D.R. "Treatment of a Bisexual Pedophile by a Biofeedback- Assisted Self-Control Procedure." **Behavior Research and Therapy**, 18(3):
207-211, 1980.

A bisexual pedophile who had molested over a thousand young boys and who had persistent sexual fantasies about young girls was treated for eighty-eight days with a biofeedback procedure which displays his erection response to sexually deviant stimuli. By using biofeedback techniques, he is able to exercise considerable self-control in his sexual responses.

201. Laws, D.R. and Pawlowski, A.V. "An Automated Fading Procedure to Alter Sexual Responsiveness in Pedophiles." **Journal of Homosexuality,** 1(2): 149-163, Winter 1974.

A nonadversive fading technique is used in the treatment of a homosexual child molester and a heterosexual child molester. Slides of children and of adults are superimposed and when the subjects produce an erection response above the designated criterion, the slide of the child fades out and the slide of the adult fades in; if the phallometric response then falls below the criterion, the fading procedure is reversed. Results show success in strengthening the sexual responses to the adult stimuli, although it is unclear as to whether the fading technique or the covert instructions the subjects gave to themselves during the process is responsible for the positive change.

202. Pinta, E.R. "Treatment of Obsessive Homosexual Pedophiliac Fantasies with Medroxyprogesterone Acetate." **Biological Psychiatry,** 13(3): 369-373, June 1978.

A significant decrease in the intensity of homosexual fantasies involving young boys is noted for a 31 year old incarcerated child molester who was given repeated doses of medroxyprogesterone acetate (Depo-Provera).

203. Serber, M. and Keith, C.G. "The Atascadero Project: Model of a Sexual Re-Training Program for Incarcerated Homosexual Pedophiles." **Journal of Homosexuality,** 1(1): 87-97, Fall 1974.

A behavioral re-training group for incarcerated homosexual child molesters teaches social interaction skills through consciousness-raising, role-playing, and assertiveness training skills.

204. Sherlock, R. and Murphy, W. "Confidentiality and Therapy: An Agency Perspective." **Comprehensive Psychiatry,** 25(1): 88-95, January/February 1984.

The case of a homosexual child molester is presented to illustrate the ethical problems that arise when the patient in a mental health agency discloses that he is involved in an on-going sexual relationship with a young boy. Several arguments for breaching confidentiality in this case are balanced against the potential harm this disclosure would have on the therapeutic process.

205. Strupp, H.H. "Some Observations on the Fallacy of Value-Free Psychotherapy and the Empty Organism: Comments on a Case Study." **Journal of Abnormal Psychology,** 83(2): 199-203, April 1974.

It is argued that no therapy is value-free and that moral values always influence even the most objective therapist's interactions with his or her patients. The Kohlenberg case study (see reference number **199**) in which a homosexual child molester is treated to achieve homosexual, rather than heterosexual, adjustment is analyzed.

206. Van Deventer, A.D. and Laws, D.R. "Orgasmic Reconditioning to Redirect Sexual Arousal in Pedophiles." **Behavior Therapy**, 9(5): 748-765, November 1978.

Two incarcerated homosexual child molesters were treated by orgasmic reconditioning techniques over an eight week period of time. Each was instructed to masturbate while saying his fantasies aloud, and the weeks each masturbated to a deviant theme were alternated with weeks of masturbation to an appropriate theme. After each session, phallometric measures were taken to stimuli of deviant and nondeviant slides. Results show that one of the homosexual child molesters showed no appreciable changes in his sexual arousal to children, while the other demonstrated a significant reduction in his arousal to children.

CHAPTER 6:
THE EFFECTS OF MOLESTATION ON CHILDREN

A great deal of reseach has been focused on the effects of sexual molestation on children. The most obvious result of that research has been the creation of "indicator lists": inventories of physical, behavioral, and emotional symptoms that are commonly found in a molested child, and that may be used, in the absence of the child's disclosure, as indicators that raise the index of suspicion that the child had been sexually molested.

Another feature of this type of research is that it begins to paint a portrait of the child at risk for sexual molestation. That one child is molested and another is not may be more than just a matter of coincidence. Some children, because of family or social circumstances or personality characteristics, seem to be more vulnerable to sexual molestation and the research has at least made tentative efforts to identify that dynamic.

Demographic Characteristics

The following references look at large samples of sexually molested children and analyze their demographic characteristics. Many of these studies also collect data on the nature of the molestation, so that important patterns and styles of interacting with the child, methods of securing the cooperation of the child, and ways to assure the secrecy of the act emerge from these demographic reports.

207. Byrne, J.P. and Valdiserri, E.V. "Victims of Childhood Sexual Abuse: A Followup Study of a Noncompliant Population." **Hospital and Community Psychiatry**, 33(11): 938-940, November 1982.
Of the 79 families referred to a hospital based therapy program when their children were sexually molested, 34 families failed to attend mandated

followup sessions. An analysis of this noncompliant group shows they do not differ in race, or in the sex of the molested child from those families that did follow through; however the average age of the molested child was slightly lower and it was more likely that the child had been sexually molested by a family member in the noncompliant families.

208. Conte, J.R. and Berliner, L. "Sexual Abuse of Children: Implications for Practice." **Social Casework,** 62(10): 601-607, December 1981.

A sample of 583 sexually molested children seen over a twenty-one month period of time at the Sexual Assault Center of the Harborview Medical Center in Seattle, Washington, is analyzed. A total of 53% of the children had been sexually molested by a person who was not related to them; slightly over half of the incidents involved some degree of physical coercion by the offending adult. Most of the children were too frightened to tell anyone about the molestation; in fact, only 16% of the children told anyone within forty-eight hours of the occurrence of the incident. Data analysis and confirmation of the children's disclosures through ancillary sources dispute the popularly held stereotype that children frequently give false reports of sexual molestation, or that incidents of sexual molestation are the products of the imaginations of children.

209. De Jong, A.R.; Emmett, G.A.; and Hervada, A.R. "Sexual Abuse of Children: Sex, Race, and Age-Dependent Variations." **American Journal of Diseases of Children**, 136(1): 129-134, February 1982.

This retrospective study examines the variables of sex, race, and age in a sample of 416 sexually molested children. Females constitute 83% of the sample; nonwhites (i.e. Blacks, Hispanics, and Orientals) comprise 79% of the sample; and most of the female children are five to six years old while the male children are six to seven years old. Physical, genital, anal, and/or psychological trauma is noted in 24% of the cases, although it is noted that the significant delays in the children's disclosures of the sexual molestation may have mitigated the signs of trauma. Those children who were sexually molested by strangers were more likely to report violence than were other children, and male children reported more violence during the course of the molestation than did the female children. Patterns that emerge in this study show that younger children have an increased risk of being sexually molested by adults who are family members or who are in some other way acquainted with the children, and have the highest rate of repeated, multiple sexual molestations prior to the medical examination. The girls are less likely to experience violence during the course of the molestation and are less likely to show symptoms of trauma. Although the sexual molestation of boys resembles that of girls in terms of dynamics and the type of sexual behavior, boys of all ages show more evidence of trauma and report more violence than do the girls.

210. Donald, T.G. "Sexual Abuse of Children in Tasmania." **Medical Journal of Australia**, 143(4): 137-138, August 19, 1985.

In 1980, sexual abuse reports to the Child Protection Department of the Australian state of Tasmania constituted only 5% of all referrals but by 1985, that figure had increased to 20%; over that five year period of time, the average age of the molested child had decreased to eight years. An analysis of referral sources shows that despite mandatory reporting laws, physicians' rate of referral remains constant at 5%, although significant increases in reporting by family members and nonprofessionals are noted.

211. Eaton, A.P. and Vastbinder, E. "The Sexually Molested Child: A Plan of Management." **Clinical Pediatrics,** 8(8): 438-441, August 1969.

A review of the medical records of 28 children referred to the emergency room of a metropolitan hospital reveals that they range in age from five months to sixteen years. All are females and six of them were sexually molested by adolescent babysitters. Suggestions for conducting the medical examination are given and it is strongly advised that laboratory testing for sexually transmitted diseases be conducted in all cases of suspected sexual molestation.

212. Farber, E.D.; Showers, J.; Johnson, C.F.; Joseph, J.A.; and Oshins, L. "The Sexual Abuse of Children: A Comparison of Male and Female Victims." **Journal of Clinical Child Psychology,** 13(3): 294-297.

The medical records of 81 sexually molested boys are compared to those of an equal number of sexually molested girls in order to determine if differences in the circumstances surrounding the molestation exist. No racial differences are noted in the composition of the two groups, and no significant differences are found in regard to the referral source, the relationship to the offending adult, the chronicity of the molestation, or in the use of bribes or threats during the molestation episode. Boys, however, are almost three times more likely to have experienced oral-genital sex than are girls. The study concludes that there are surprisingly few differences in the circumstances surrounding the molestation of boys compared to that of girls.

213. Grant, L.J. "Assessment of Child Sexual Abuse: Eighteen Months Experience at the Child Protection Center." **American Journal of Obstetrics and Gynecology,** 148(5): 617-620, March 1984.

The records of 157 cases of child sexual abuse referred to the Children's Hospital's Child Protection Center in Manitoba, Canada are reviewed. The children range in age from eight months to seventeen years, and 13% of the cases are those of young boys. No peak day of the week for referrals is noted and most cases are referred during regular working hours. Sexually transmitted diseases are found in 9.5% of the cases.

214. Hayman, C.R.; Lewis, F.R.; Stewart, W.F.; and Grant, M. "A Public Health Program for Sexually Assaulted Females." **Public Health Reports,** 82(6): 497-504, June 1967.

An analysis of 335 complaints of sexual assault seen at a Washington, D.C. hospital reveals that 89 are children under the age of fourteen. Few of these children had experienced any physical trauma along with the molestation, but most of them showed some signs of emotional trauma. The follow-up service conducted by public health nurses is also described.

215. Hayman, C.R.; Stewart, W.F.; Lewis, F.R.; and Grant, M. "Sexual Assault on Women and Children in the District of Columbia." **Public Health Reports,** 83(12): 1021-1028, December 1968.

Of the 451 sexual assault cases referred to a Washington, D.C. hospital, 23.5% involve children under the age of twelve years.

216. Jaffe, A.C.; Dynneson, L.; and ten Besel, R.W. "Sexual Abuse of Children: An Epidemiologic Study." **American Journal of Diseases of Children,** 129(6): 689-692, June 1975.

An epidemiologic summary of 291 cases of sexually molested children shows that indecent liberties were taken with 39% of the children; 6% were raped; other types of sexual contact occurred with 7% of the children; and the remainder were approached by men who indecently exposed themselves. Half of all of these cases occurred between the months of May and September, and half occurred between the hours of 2 p.m. and 6 p.m. The children range in age from two to fifteen years, with a mean age of 10.7 years.

217. Jason, J.; Williams, S.L.; Burton, A.; and Rochat, R. "Epidemiologic Difference Between Sexual and Physical Child Abuse." **Journal of the American Medical Association,** 247(24): 3344-3348, June 25, 1982.

The cases of 735 sexually molested children referred to the Georgia Department of Protective Services are compared to cases of 3,486 physically molested children. Analysis shows that sexually molested children are more likely to be female, are younger, have fewer physical injuries, and are less likely to require hospitalization than the physically abused children.

218. Kahn, M. and Sexton, M. "Sexual Abuse of Young Children." **Clinical Pediatrics,** 22(5): 369-372, May 1983.

Over an eighteen month period of time, all cases of child sexual abuse treated at the Pediatric Outpatient Clinic at the University of Maryland School of Medicine were referred to a social work team for analysis and the collection of data. A sample of 113 referred children below the age of twelve shows that 56% had been sexually molested by a nonfamily person. A variety of behavioral and emotional problems are documented for the children who also have a high rate of sexually transmitted diseases. The molesters were male in 93% of the cases, and most of the children in this sample are female. Speculations about biases that may preclude the identification of sexually molested young boys are also offered.

219. Kercher, G. and McShane, M. "Characterizing Child Sexual Abuse on the Basis of a Multi-Agency Sample." **Victimology: An International Journal,** 9(3-4): 364-382, 1984.

An analysis of 1108 cases of child molestation referred to Children's Protective Services and the District Attorney's office of Harris County, Texas shows that the average age of the referred child is 10.8 years, and that girls outnumber boys five to one, although boys are three times more likely to have been molested by a nonfamily person. Slightly less than half of the cases are extrafamilial and in almost all of those cases, the perpetrator is the same race as the child.

220. Landis, J.T. "Experiences of 500 Children with Adult Sexual Deviants." **Psychiatric Quarterly Supplement**, 30(1): 91-109, 1956.

Results of a questionnaire inquiring about family background are compared between 500 adults who reported a history of sexual molestation during childhood, with 450 adults who did not. Males who had been sexually molested differed from nonmolested males on two variables: they were more likely to be sexually active at the time of the study, and they had started dating earlier. Females who had been sexually molested differed from nonmolested females on five variables: they described more distant relationships with their mothers; they were more likely to have a mother who worked outside of the home; their fathers were more likely to work in semi-skilled or unskilled jobs; they were more likely to be sexually active at the time of the study; and they were more likely to have experienced orgasm before marriage. Finally, females with a history of childhood molestation could be divided into "accidental" and "participant" victims, the latter having in various ways brought on, encouraged, or seduced the molestation. When these two groups are compared, the participant victims are found to have had more family problems and more strained relationships with parents than is found for the accidental victims.

221. Law, S.K. "Child Molestation: A Comparison of Hong Kong and Western Findings." **Medicine, Science and the Law,** 19(1): 55-60, January 1979.

A retrospective review of 155 heterosexual and homosexual child molesters referred for psychiatric evaluation in Hong Kong reveals that they differ slightly from those child molesters described in American studies. The Hong Kong sample tends to be younger, has less education, lower intelligence, and is more likely to have been diagnosed as mentally ill. Few differences are found between the molested children of Hong Kong and the molested children described in American studies.

222. Mannarino, A.P. and Cohen, J.A. "A Clinical-Demographic Study of Sexually Abused Children." **Child Abuse and Neglect,** 10(1): 17-23, 1986.

The aim of this study is to provide clinical and demographic data on sexually molested children to challenge some of the widely held assumptions that appear in the literature. The subjects are 45 sexually molested children, ages three to sixteen; they come from all socioeconomic classes and 30% of them are Black. All of the children were given intelligence tests and results show a mean I.Q. of 92.9 points. The vast majority of the children experienced fondling; 11% experienced vaginal, oral, or rectal intercourse. Although none of the children had been physically forced into the act, 17% did report having been threatened by the molester. The parents of the children were asked to fill out a symptom checklist and 69% of the children display at least one symptom. Nightmares are most commonly reported; anxiety, clinging behavior, and feelings of sadness are also common; enuresis occurred for some of the children as did inappropriate sexual behaviors.

223. Pierce, R. and Pierce, L.H. "The Sexually Abused Child: A Comparison of Male and Female Victims." **Child Abuse and Neglect,** 9(2): 191-199, 1985.

Of the 205 confirmed cases of child molestation reported to a child abuse hotline between 1976 and 1979, 12% of the cases involve male children. A review of the hotline records shows that 20% of these males had been sexually molested by a nonfamily person, compared to 6% of the female children. As a group, the males are younger, are less likely to have a father-figure in the home, were more likely to experience oral sex during the molestation, and were more likely to have been threatened by the molester than were the female children. Although males were referred for therapy as often as females were, they were in therapy for a shorter period of time.

224. Rimsza, M.E. and Niggemann, E.H. "Medical Evaluation of Sexually Abused Children: A Review of 311 Cases." **Pediatrics,** 69(1): 8-14, January 1982.

Patient characteristics, types of sexual molestation, physical examination findings and laboratory data are reviewed in the hospital charts of 311 sexually molested children. The goal of the review is to obtain enough data to make clinically relevant recommendations regarding the diagnosis and the medical management of these cases. The children range in age from two months to seventeen years, with a mean age of 9.2 years. The molester was known to the child in 75% of the cases, and in 6% of the cases, there were multiple molesters. Single episodes of molestation are reported by 51% of the children; the remainder experienced multiple molestations over a period of time that ranged from one week to nine years. The children's reticence to disclose the episodes is reflected in the fact that only 45% of them were medically examined within three days of the incident; factors such as the fear of punishment, of not being believed, of being abandoned or rejected, as well as the secondary gains of gifts and favors are believed to underlie these delays in disclosures.

225. Scherzer, L.N. and Lala, P. "Sexual Offenses Committed Against Children." **Clinical Pediatrics,** 19(10): 679-685, October 1980.

An analysis of 73 cases of children under the age of fourteen who were referred to Baltimore City Hospital for sexual molestation shows that half of them had experienced sexual intercourse, and half of them had been taken to the hospital within the twenty-four hours after the molestation. Most of the children were Black and were living in single parent families that were receiving some kind of public assistance. The difficulties of treating children from economically deprived families are discussed, and the stresses on these families that may render their children vulnerable to sexual molestation are analyzed.

226. Sedney, M.A. and Brooks, B. "Factors Associated with a History of Childhood Sexual Experiences in a Nonclinical Female Population." **Journal of the American Academy of Child Psychiatry,** 23(2): 215-218, March 1984.

A survey of 301 female college students as to any childhood sexual experiences reveals that 16% had experienced sexual contact during their childhood, most of them with family members. These respondents were then compared to a control group of nonmolested female college students and results show that the molested females report more disruptive symptoms in their adult lives. The most commonly reported symptoms are depression, sleep problems, anxiety, thoughts of hurting oneself, and vulnerability to further criminal victimization.

227. Shah, C.P.; Holloway, C.P.; and Valkil, D.V. "Sexual Abuse of Children." **Annals of Emergency Medicine,** 11(1): 18-23, January 1982.

A retrospective review of the cases of 843 sexually molested children treated at a hospital emergency room shows that the children ranged in age from twenty-three days to eighteen years, with a mean age of 10 years; 90% of the children are girls. A detailed analysis of 174 of the most recently referred cases reveals that most of them knew their assailant; 40% of them had experienced sexual intercourse; and only 8% of them also experienced physical injury in conjunction with the molestation. The procedures for taking a complete history, conducting a medical examination, and collecting physical evidence for possible future criminal proceedings also are discussed.

228. Shamroy, J.A. "A Perspective on Childhood Sexual Abuse." **Social Work,** 25(2): 128-131, March 1980.

A total of 78 children under the age of thirteen was treated for sexual molestation at the Children's Hospital Medical Center in Cincinnati in 1977. Analysis of the sample shows that 65% had been sexually molested by a non-family person.

229. Tilelli, J.A.; Turek, D.; and Jaffe, A.C. "Sexual Abuse of Children: Clinical Findings and Implications for Management." **New England Journal of Medicine,** 302(6): 319-323, February 1980.

A retrospective study of the hospital records of 130 sexually molested children between the ages of two and sixteen years old, and with a mean age of 11.3 years, reveals that 33% of the children showed signs of physical trauma that includes bruises and lacerations. The children were acquainted with the molester in 64% of the cases; those remaining children who were molested by strangers are significantly younger than those molested by an acquaintance or family member. Referrals for counseling were made in 87% of the cases.

230. Virkkunen, M. "Victim-Precipitated Pedophilia Offenses." **British Journal of Criminology,** 15(2): 175-180, April 1975.

A review of the cases of 64 hospitalized Finnish child molesters reveals that in 48% of the cases, the children they molested initiated or otherwise brought on the sexual molestation incident, according to the descriptions of the offenses given by the molesters. When compared to children who did not initiate the molestation, these "precipitating children" tend more often to be of limited intellectual capacity and/or mentally ill, but are less likely than the other children to have been adjudicated as delinquent.

Medical Examination

The necessity of conducting a complete and careful medical examination of children when sexual molestation is alleged or suspected is strongly emphasized in the literature. Just as important as that medical examination is, it is also difficult to conduct because of the developmental immaturity of the children and their discomfort and fear of such procedures.

The following references outline and explain the procedures for conducting the examination and stress the physical symptoms and signs that are often found in sexually molested children.

231. Branch, G. and Paxton, R. "A Study of Gonococcal Infections Among Infants and Children." **American Journal of Diseases of Children,** 80(4): 347-352, April 1965.
The records of 180 children under the age of 15 years who were discovered upon medical examination to have gonorrhea are reviewed in order to ascertain the source of this sexually transmitted disease. Although most of the children contracted gonorrhea through sexual contact with a relative, 18% were infected through molestation by a nonfamily person.

232. Breen, J.L.; Greenwald, E.; and Gregori, C.A. "The Molested Young Female." **Pediatric Clinics of North America,** 19(3): 717-725, 1972.
The physician's role in the medical evaluation of sexually molested female children is discussed.

233. (Comment). "Herpes From Abuse." **Emergency Medicine,** 17(9): 79-81, May 15, 1985.
Genital herpes has an incubation period of two to twenty days and can manifest either locally or systemically, so it is not always clinically evident upon initial referral. In cases of suspected sexual molestation, a herpes titer along with cultures for gonorrhea and a serologic test for syphillis should be conducted, and the parents of the child should be advised to watch for vesicles on the genitals and tender lymph nodes in the groin. A followup medical examination two weeks later, and another eight weeks later, can medically confirm the presence of genital herpes.

234. (Comment). "A Protocol for Managing the Sexually Abused Child." **Emergency Medicine,** 17(10): 59-60, 63-64, 72, May 30, 1985.

The protocol for the use of a multidisciplinary team for the medical evaluation of sexually molested children is described.

235. DeJong, A.R.; Weiss, J.C.; and Brent, R.L. "Condyloma Acuminata in Children." **American Journal of Diseases of Children,** 136(7): 704-706, July 1982.

Condyloma acuminata, or venereal warts, is being seen with greater frequency in recent years in prepubertal children. Transmission of this sexually transmitted disease may occur during delivery, sexual contact, or nonsexual contact within the family. Four new cases are presented, one of which was contracted during an incident of sexual molestation. A review of the literature uncovers thirty reported cases, 23% of which came from sexual contact, and 57% from unknown sources. It is hypothesized that sexual contact may be the primary mode of transmission and that examining physicians must enhance their interviewing skills with children in order to determine the source of this sexually transmitted disease.

236. DeJong, A.R. "Vaginitis Due to Gardnerella Vaginalis and to Candida Albicans in Sexual Abuse." **Child Abuse and Neglect,** 9(1): 27-29, 1985.

Candida albicans and Gardnerella vaginalis should not be considered normal flora when found in symptomatic children, and the possibility of sexual molestation must be considered. Two cases of young children who contracted these sexually transmitted diseases during incidents of sexual molestation are presented.

237. DeJong, A.R. "The Medical Evaluation of Sexual Abuse in Children." **Hospital and Community Psychiatry,** 36(5): 509-512, May 1985.

The overall objectives of any medical intervention strategy with a sexually molested child include identification, management of acute medical problems, determination of the history of the sexual assault, management of any acute emotional problems of the child and/or family, the protection of the child against further molestation incidents, the development of treatment followup plans, and the compliance with legal requirements regarding the collection of evidence, the obligation to report, and the possibility of future court testimony. Physicians should suspect child molestation if there is evidence of sexually transmitted disease; vaginal or rectal lacerations, abrasions, or bruises; pregnancy; a history of physical abuse or sexual abuse; hematuria; behavioral problems; or dysuria. A young child's disclosure of sexual molestation should be believed, especially if the child discusses multiple episodes, a progression in sexual acts over time, elements of secrecy, and explicit details. The lack of training in this area, the stress the discovery of molestation produces, and the frustration with interactions with the social service delivery network are factors that contribute to physicans' failure to recognize child molesation and/or to report it.

238. Dershewitz, R.A.; Levitsky, L.L.; and Feingold, M. "Vulvovaginitis: A Case of Clitorimegaly." **American Journal of Diseases of Children,** 138(9): 887-888, September 1984.

The case of an eight year old girl who had vulvovaginitis with an en-
larged clitoris and multiple vulvar vesicles as a result of sexual molestation
is presented.

239. Elvik, S.L.; Berkowitz, C.D.; and Greenberg, C.S. "Child Sexual Abuse:
The Role of the Nurse Practitioner." **Nurse Practitioner: The American
Journal of Primary Health Care,** 11(1): 15-22, January 1986.
The role of the nurse practitioner in the examination of a sexually molested child is delineated. A progressive head-to-toe medical examination is
recommended as is the use of Tanner staging to assess the child's stage of
sexual maturity. Transections or tears of the hymenal orifice located between eleven and one o'clock are usually indicative of digital penetration;
transections between five and seven o'clock usually occur as a result of penetration. Any synechiae, or adhesions from healing transections, should also
be noted; and any thickening of the hymen is likely to have occurred because of repeated sexual trauma. Sodomy usually produces a paradoxic relaxation of the anal sphincter, and a loss of contraction upon gentle stroking
of the perianal skin. Other possible signs, such as anal fissures, skin tags,
loss of adiposity in the perianal area, or a thickening of the skin around the
anus also should be noted.

240. Everett, R.B. and Jimerson, G.F. "The Rape Victim: A Review of 117
Consecutive Cases." **Obstetrics and Gynecology,** 50(1): 88-90, July 1977.
The hospital charts of 117 rape victims, 22% of whom were children,
were reviewed. Techniques for conducting the medical examinations of
these patients are discussed.

241. Farrell, M.K.; Billmire, M.E.; Shamroy, J.A.; and Hammond, J.G. "Prepubertal Gonorrhea: A Multidisciplinary Team Approach." **Pediatrics,** 69(1):
151-153, January 1981.
All children under the age of twelve years with suspected gonorrhea
are interviewed by a multidisciplinary team to determine the mode of transmission of this sexually transmitted disease. The history of exposure was
elicited from 32 of the 46 children interviewed: 59% contracted the gonorrhea through incidents of sexual molestation, but only a small proportion of
all children will voluntarily disclose the history of molestation upon initial
evaluation. It is recommended that a multidisciplinary team be used to
evaluate and interview these children and that the children be hospitalized
to facilitate the evaluation process.

242. Folland, D.S.; Burke, R.E.; Hinman, A.R.; and Schaffner, W. "Gonorrhea
in Preadolescent Children: An Inquiry into Source of Infection and Mode of
Transmission." **Pediatrics,** 60(2): 153-156, August 1977.
A study of 73 children under the age of ten years with gonorrhea reveals that sexual molestation may have been the source of this sexually
transmitted disease for 12% of the sample.

243. Fore. C.V. and Holmes, S.S. "Sexual Abuse of Children." **Nursing Clinics of North America,** 19(2): 329-340, June 1984.

In assessing whether a child has been sexually molested, nurses are advised to take a complete history which covers developmental issues for the child, the current family structure and home setting, the names and relationships of current caregivers, past injuries and illnesses, and the presence of any symptomatology that may be indicative of sexual molestation. The use of play techniques and drawings are encouraged to facilitate the evaluation process.

244. Furniss, T.; Bingley-Miller, L.; and Bentovim, A. "Therapeutic Approach to Sexual Abuse." **Archive of Diseases in Childhood,** 59(9): 865-870, September 1984.

Presenting symptoms of sexually molested children may include sexually transmitted diseases; genital or rectal itching, bleeding, or discharge; recurrent urinary tract infections; enuresis; sleeping and eating disorders; recurrent abdominal pains; secretiveness; withdrawal; self-injuring behavior; and somatic complaints.

245. Gorline, L.L. and Ray, M.M. "Examining and Caring for the Child Who Has Been Sexually Assaulted." **American Journal of Maternal/ Child Nursing,** 4(2): 110-114, March/April 1979.

Guidelines for the nurse who is conducting a preliminary medical examination of a sexually molested child are presented. Visual inspection of the labia majora should look for any redness, bruising, or marks. Rupture or scarring of the hymen should be noted, and the urethra and anus should also be examined. Evidence should be collected with the use of a standard rape kit.

246. Groothuis, J.R.; Bischoff, M.C.; and Jauregui, L.E. "Pharyngeal Gonorrhea in Young Children." **Pediatric Infectious Diseases,** 2(2): 99-101, March/April 1983.

A retrospective study of the medical records of all children seen at a pediatric clinic of a large metropolitan hospital reveals that 16 of them presented a complaint of sexual molestation. Pharyngeal, anal, and genital cultures were obtained for these children, and positive cultures for pharyngeal gonorrhea are found for 44% of those children. Since none of those children was symptomatic, physicians are encouraged to take routine pharyngeal cultures in cases of suspected child molestation.

247. Hammerschlag, M.R.; Doraiswamy, B.; Russell, A.E.; Cox, P.; Price, W.; and Gleyzer, A. "Are Rectogenital Chlamydial Infections a Marker of Sexual Abuse in Children?" **Pediatric Infectious Diseases,** 3(2): 100-104, March/April 1984.

The cultures of 51 sexually molested children were compared to those of 43 controls. Chlamydia trachomatis is isolated in the vaginas and rectums of two of the molested children, and three of the controls. The results suggest that cultures for this infection should routinely be given to children who present a complaint of sexual molestation, but that positive results in any child should not be taken to mean that the molestation was recent.

248. Hammerschlag, M.R.; Cummings, M.; Doraiswamy, B.; Cox, P.; and McCormack, W.M. "Nonspecific Vaginitis Following Sexual Abuse in Children." **Pediatrics,** 75(6): 1028-1031, June 1985.

Nonspecific vaginitis is a polymicrobial infection that is the most common casue of vaginitis in adults. To determine whether it is more common in sexually molested children, 31 children were given vaginal washes and the wash was examined for clue cells and odor that are both symptoms of nonspecific vaginitis; the results were compared to the vaginal washings of 23 children who had not been molested. Test results show that only one of the molested children showed immediate symptoms of nonspecific vaginitis; however eight additional children developed symptoms after one week. Only one of the non-molested children showed symptoms. The necessity of incorporating this procedure into the medical examination of sexually molested children is stressed.

249. Hayman, C.R. and Lanza, C. "Sexual Assault on Women and Girls." **American Journal of Obstetrics and Gynecology,** 109(3): 480-486, February 1971.

A retrospective review of 2190 sexual assault cases referred to a Washington, D.C. hospital shows that 11% of them involved children under the age of twelve years, and that the examining physicians in general did a poor job in assessing the emotional conditions of the children, and in making referrals for on-going therapy. An aggressive follow-up program conducted by public health nurses assists in the identification of children with emotional problems and facilitates the referral of the children for counseling.

250. Hayman, C.R. and Lanza, C. "Victimology of Sexual Assault." **Medical Aspects of Human Sexuality,** 5(10): 152, 161, October 1971.

The role of medical personnel in the evaluations and interviews of children who have been sexually molested is discussed in this brief article.

251. Hayman, C.R.; Lewis, F.R.; Stewart, W.F.; and Grant, M. "A Public Health Program for Sexually Molested Females." **Public Health Reports,** 82(6): 497-504, June 1967.

A retrospective review of 322 cases of sexual assault referred to a city hospital reveals that 23.6% of the cases involved children under the age of twelve years. The details of the medical examination procedure, the testing for sexually transmitted diseases, and the referral processes are given.

252. Herjanic, B. "Medical Symptoms of Sexual Abuse of Children." **Medical Aspects of Human Sexuality,** 12(9): 139-140, September 1978.

Physicians examining sexually molested children should look for vaginal or urethral discharges, oral fissures, stridor or choking symptoms in infants or very young children, complaints of pain upon defecation, and other generalized evidence of abuse which may include fractures, bites, bruises, and burns. Evidence of behavioral symptoms such as unusual fears, nonspecific psychological symptoms like guilt, depression, anxiety and irritability; and unusual sexual acting out also may be indicative of sexual molestation.

253. Herjanic, B. and Wilbois, R.P. "Sexual Abuse of Children: Detection and Management." **Journal of the American Medical Association,** 239(4): 331-333, January 1978.

A high index of suspicion is needed to detect child molestation. Suspicions should be raised by findings of vaginal or penile discharge, lesions around the mouth or perineum, dysuria, painful defecation, perineal itching, unexplained choking on mucous-like secretions, and/or the presence of a sexually transmitted disease. Procedures for doing pelvic examinations on young girls are noted, and the procedure for the collection of physical evidence is discussed.

254. Hogan, W.L. "The Raped Child." **Medical Aspects of Human Sexuality,** 8(11): 129-130, November 1974.

The medical examination of the raped child should begin as a general exam with a gradual transition to the genital area. Descriptive analysis of the genital area should include the parous or vaginal nature of the intoitus; a description of any pubertal changes; the presence of overt lacerations with bleeding; subepithelial or petechial hemorrhages of the labia; generalized or localized erythema at the entrances of the vagina or in the vicinity of the fourchette; the presence of mucoid exudate in the vaginal vault; the appearance of the anus or anorectal region; the characteristics of the hymenal ring; and the presence or absence of true menstruation.

255. Hunter, R.S.; Kilstrom, N.; and Loda, F. "Sexually Abused Children: Identifying Masked Presentations in a Medical Setting." **Child Abuse and Neglect,** 9(1): 17-25, 1985.

It is theorized that some child molestation goes undetected by hospital personnel because the children both present a wide array of symptoms that mask its presence and do not immediately disclose the molestation to anyone. To test this hypothesis, 50 children with masked presentations are compared to 31 overt cases. The children in these two groups do not differ significantly in age and both groups tend to come from high risk families. Those with masked presentations tend to display a wider variety of symptomatology that includes genital complaints, sexually transmitted diseases, pregnancy, psychosomatic complaints, and behavior problems. When compared to the overt group, the children with masked presentations are twice as likely to have a history of chronic sexual abuse, and three times as likely to have a history of school problems or psychosomatic disorders. The presence of these masked cases suggests that child molestation may be at least twice as common as the number of overt cases would lead medical personnel to believe. Physicans are encouraged to carefully evaluate symptoms even if the child fails to disclose the molestation or refuses to acknowledge it. A medical team approach is found to be especially helpful in both identifying these cases and in providing medical intervention and referral.

256. Ingram, D.L.; White, S.T.; Durfee, M.F.; and Peterson, A.W. "Sexual Contact in Children with Gonorrhea." **American Journal of Diseases of Children**, 136(11): 994-996, November 1982.

To test the hypothesis that gonorrhea in children one to twelve years old is frequently associated with sexual contact, the medical records and histories of 31 infected children are examined. Few of the children, upon initial examination. had named or identified the persons who had had sexual contact with them; however, when 100 extended family members and caretakers of these children were given cultures, 35% either had gonorrhea or had been treated for it in the previous several weeks. After these people have been identified, supplemental interviews with the children reveal histories of sexual contacts for fourteen additional cases. The study supports the hypothesis that sexual contact is the source of virtually all cases of gonorrhea in children, and warns medical personnel that children tend to be reticent about disclosing the source of the infection upon initial evaluation.

257. Jones, J.G. "Sexual Abuse of Children: Current Concepts." **American Journal of Diseases of Children,** 136(2): 142-146, February 1982.

Guidelines for interviewing sexually molested children and for conducting medical examinations are presented.

258. Jones, J.G.; Yamauchi, T.; and Lambert, B. "Trichomonas Vaginalis Infestation in Sexually Abused Girls." **American Journal of Diseases of Children**, 139(8): 846-847, August 1985.

Four cases of sexually molested girls who had contracted trichomonas vaginalis are presented.

259. Kaplan, K.M.; Fleisher, G.R.; Paradise, J.E.; and Friedman, H.N. "Social Relevance of Genital Herpes Simplex in Children." **American Journal of Dieases of Children**, 138(9): 872-874, September 1984.

Six cases of children who had genital herpes were found in this retrospective study of hospital records. Sexual molestation was confirmed as the source of the infections for four of the children; the source was unconfirmed in the other two. Physicians are advised to consider the possiblity that a child with genital herpes has been sexually molested.

260. Kirschner, R.H. and Stein, R.J. "The Mistaken Diagnosis of Child Abuse: A Form of Medical Abuse?" **American Journal of Diseases of Children,** 139(9): 873-875, September 1985.

Ten cases of mistaken diagnosis of abuse in children who had died are presented; three cases involve children who showed gaping of the rectum and vagina and were incorrectly diagnosed as having been sexually molested. All of the cases are due to misinterpretations of postmortem changes in the bodies of children.

261. Lipton, G.L. and Roth, E.I. "Rape: A Complex Management Problem in the Pediatric Emergency Room." **Journal of Pediatrics,** 75(5): 859-866, November 1969.

The details of 9 cases of child rape brought to a hospital emergency room are presented. In all of the cases, the complaint of the alleged rape can be perceived as a symptom of a preexisting disturbance in the children's psychosexual development and/or family life. Some degree of unconscious complicity with the molester is noted in 33% of the children. None of the cases show serious physical or emotional trauma.

262. Massey, J.B.; Garcia, C.R.; and Emrich, J.P. "Management of Sexually Assaulted Females." **Obstetrics and Gynecology**, 38(1): 29-36, July 1971.
The procedures for the medical examinations of 479 sexual assault cases, 24% of whom were children, are reviewed. .

263. McCoy, C.R.; Applebaum, H.; and Besser, A. "Condyloma Acuminata: An Unusual Presentation of Child Abuse." **Journal of Pediatric Surgery**, 17(5): 505-507, October 1982.
The presence of Condyloma acuminata in young children should indicate the possibility of sexual abuse; physicians are advised to inquire about a history of molestation in children with this sexually transmitted disease.

264. Mian, M.; Wehrspann, W.; Klajner-Diamond, H.; LaBaron, D.; and Winder, C. "Review of 125 Children Six Years of Age and Under Who Were Sexually Abused." **Child Abuse and Neglect**, 10(2): 223-229, 1986.
A retrospective review of the hospital records of 125 sexually molested children six years of age and under reveals that 36% of them had been molested by a nonfamily person. Most of the children had experienced fondling at the hands of a person previously acquainted with them. Most of the children displayed some symptomatology upon admission with vaginal discharge, bruises in the genital and buttocks area, sexually transmitted diseases, and/or abdominal pain being the most commonly reported. Emotional symptoms such as nightmares, clinging behavior, fearfulness, and sexually inappropriate behavior and/or language were also frequently reported. Children who were molested by a nonfamily person were more likely to purposefully disclose the incident; "accidental" disclosure, that is, discovery of the molestation through third party observations, medical symptomatology in the children, or through the sexualized behavior of the children, occurred more often in cases of incest.

265. Orr, D.P. "Management of Childhood Sexual Abuse." **Journal of Family Practice**, 11(7): 1057-1064, 1980.
A plan to manage the sexually abused child in the emergency room is presented. The evaluation must begin with the identification of the sexual abuse; this may come through a complaint, through relevant symptomatology, or through such nonspecific symptoms as behavioral disturbances. The medical examination should begin as a general exam and then proceed to the inspection of the external genitalia. Any abnormalities, particularly skin marks, should be noted as to size, color, and location. Abrasions, erythema, fissures, and/or the presence of semen in the rectal area also should be noted. The hymenal opening and size should be estimated in girls and if there

is sign of genital trauma, an examination of the entire vaginal vault and peri-cervical area must be conducted. Stains and cultures for sexually transmitted diseases should be taken and serologic tests for syphillis are also recommended. The examination of boys should include gentle pressure on the penile urethra; pain or discharge would indicate urethritis which could be indicative of sexual molestation.

266. Orr, D.P. and Prietto, S.V. "Emergency Management of Sexually Abused Children." **American Journal of Diseases of Children,** 133(6): 628-631, June 1979.

One hundred children brought into a hospital emergency room for suspected sexual molestation show a variety of symptoms that include vaginal discharge, bleeding or lacerations; vulvar erythema; ecchymosis; and sexually transmitted diseases. Suggestions for conducting the medical examination are offered and the development of hospital protocol for dealing with such cases is discussed. Medical personnel are also advised to note that some children are asymptomatic; in fact, 65% of the girls in this sample had normal findings on the physical examination.

267. Paradise, J.E.; Campos, J.M.; Friedman, H.M.; and Frismuth, G. "Vulvo-vaginitis in Premenarcheal Girls: Clinical Features and Diagnostic Evaluation." **Pediatrics,** 70(2): 193-198, August 1982.

The cultures of the vaginal secretions of 54 young girls with symptoms of vulvovaginitis were compared to those of an age-matched control group. Vaginal discharge is found in 48% of the symptomatic girls and in none of the control group. Although the most common cause of vulvovaginitis is poor hygiene, 11% of the girls with it had been sexually molested. The examining physician is advised to make specific inquiries about a history of sexual molestation of children in whom this disorder is diagnosed.

268. Paul, D.M. "The Medical Exam in Sexual Offenses Against Children." **Medicine, Science and the Law,** 17:251-258, 1977.

Labial tears, circumferential tears of the vestibular mucosa and posterior hymen tears are frequently found in the medical examination of children under the age of ten who have experienced attempted penetration; full penetration also can cause anterior tears in the bladder, bruising of the vaginal walls, and rupture of the vaginal vault. Anorectal sexual assualts in children frequently do not cause gross anal injuries, although the size of the penetrating object, the frequency of the assaults, and the use of force are variables which may change that finding. Laxity of the anal sphincter, swelling and hematoma of the anal verge, and fissures and tears of the anal sphincter are the most commonly found indications of anorectal assault in children.

269. Rettig, P.J. and Nelson, J.D. "Genital Tract Infection with Chlamydia Trachomatis in Prepubertal Children." **Journal of Pediatrics,** 99(2): 206-210, August 1981.

Thirty-one children with gonococcal anogenital infection were examined and compared to 23 children with nongonococcal urethritis and vaginitis. Chlamydia trachomatis was found in 29% of the first group and in none of the control group. The finding of chlamydia trachomatis and gonococcal infection in prepubertal children should raise the suspicion of a history of sexual molestation.

270. Ricci, L.R. "Child Sexual Abuse: The Emergency Department Response." **Annals of Emergency Medicine,** 15(6): 711-716, June 1986.
The stages of conducting a thorough medical examination in cases of suspected child molestation are delineated. A brief history should be taken, and a thorough genital/rectal examination must be conducted. Stains and cultures to test for sexually transmitted diseases are an essential part of the examination. Evidence should be collected in the event that the case will come to criminal trial and a comprehensive treatment and follow-up plan must be developed for each child.

271. Rosenfeld, A.A. "The Clinical Management of Incest and Sexual Abuse of Children." **Journal of the American Medical Association,** 242(16): 1761-1764, October 1979.
Clues to the sexual molestation of children include genital complaints, sexually transmitted diseases, and reports of compulsive masturbation, sexual acting out, and any unpredictable and extreme alterations in behavior.

272. Roth, E.I. "Emergency Treatment of Raped Children." **Medical Aspects of Human Sexuality,** 6(8): 85-91, August 1972.
Problems in the emergency treatment of raped children are outlined. Techniques for conducting the medical examination and for assessing the degree of the emotional impact of the molestation experience are discussed.

273. Ryan, M.T. "Identifying the Sexually Abused Child." **Pediatric Nursing,** 10(6): 419-421, November/December 1984.
Physical indicators of sexual molestation in children include sexually transmitted diseases; vaginal or rectal bleeding; pain or itching in the genital area; foreign bodies in the vagina, rectum or urethra; stretched or lacerated hymen; pain upon urination; pregnancy; and inflammation of the urethra or inguinal lymph glands. Nurses should also look for such behavioral indicators as regressive behavior, sexually precocious behavior, depression, anxiety, and psychosomatic complaints. Interviewing skills for nurses are also discussed.

274. Sadan, O.; Koller, A.B.; Adno, A.; and Beale, P.G. "Massive Vulval Condylomata Acuminata in a Ten Month Old Child with Suspected Sexual Abuse: Case Report." **British Journal of Obstetrics and Gynecology,** 92(11): 1201-1203, November 1985.
The case of a ten month old girl admitted for surgery because of massive condylomata acuminata covering her entire vulval area and extending into the anal region is presented. The child had contracted the disease from sexual molestation.

275. Seidel, J.; Zonana, J.; and Totten, E. "Condylomata Acuminata as a Sign of Sexual Abuse in Children." **Journal of Pediatrics,** 95(4): 553-554, October 1979.

When Condylomata acuminata is found in prepubescent children, sexual molestation should be the suspected mode of transmission. A medical examination should include cultures of the pharynx, rectum, and vagina. Four cases are presented in detail.

276. Seidl, T. and Paradise, J.E. "Child Sexual Abuse: Effective Case Management by a Multidisciplinary Team." **Medical Times,** 112(8): 3-6, August 1984.

A team management approach for the diagnosis, medical examination, and referral of sexually molested children is described.

277. Sgroi, S.M. "Kids with Clap: Gonorrhea as an Indicator of Child Sexual Assault." **Victimology: An International Journal,** 2(2): 251-267, Summer 1977.

Gonorrhea infections in children in any body site except the eyes is a tell-tale indicator of child molestation. The examination of the child in cases where sexual molestation is suspected should include a complete physical and developmental examination; skeletal x-rays for children under six years old; a genital examination with a vaginal smear; cultures of the throat, urethra, rectum, and vagina, as well as blood tests to screen for venereal diseases.

278. Shore, W.B. and Winkelstein, J.A. "Nonvenereal Transmission of Gonococcal Infections to Children." **Journal of Pediatrics,** 79(4): 661-663, October 1971.

The purpose of this study is to alert physicians to an increasing incidence of gonococcal infections in children, and to the possibility that such infections can be transmitted in such nonsexual ways as touching an object, or lying in sheets or blankets contaminated by the gonococcal infection. Nonsexual modes of transmission are suggested based on a review of the medical records of 14 infected children between the ages of six weeks and twelve years old. Since only three of these children disclosed having been sexually molested to medical personnel, other modes of transmission of the infection must be considered.

279. Slager-Jorne, P. "Counseling Sexually Abused Children." **Personnel and Guidance Journal,** 57(2): 103-105, October 1978.

Five cases of sexually molested children are presented. Each experienced anxiety which created phobias, tics, nightmares, enuresis, eating disorders and sexual acting out. Therapists are encouraged to create a supportive, understanding environment in which presenting symptoms are treated until the child is able and willing to discuss the sexual molestation.

280. Soules, M.R.; Stewart, S.K.; Brown, K.M.; and Pollard, A. "The Spectrum of Alleged Rape." **Journal of Reproductive Medicine,** 20(1): 33-39, January 1978.

Hospital protocol for the examination of child and adult rape victims is outlined. The medical examination should include a general physical examination, a pelvic examination, a semen test, an acid phosphatose test, and a screen for ABO blood group antigens. Advice is also given for handling physical evidence for later presentation in a criminal trial.

281. Terrell, M.E. "Identifying the Sexually Abused Child in a Medical Setting." **Health and Social Work,** 2(4): 112-130, November 1977.

This retrospective study of the hospital records of 36 patients under the age of eleven who were treated for gonococcal infections of the genitourinary tract shows that sexual molestation is not always asked about or investigated as the possible source of the infection. Hospital staff are urged to do complete medical exams and lab tests for sexually transmitted diseases in all cases of suspected child molestation, and to familiarize themselves with the medical and psychological symptoms frequently associated with molestation.

282. Thomas, J.N. "Yes, You Can Help a Sexually Abused Child." **RN,** 43(8): 23-29, August 1980.

On the basis of the medical examinations of 500 sexually molested children, 300 of whom were molested by a nonfamily person, the following symptoms are most commonly noted: sexually transmitted diseases; vaginal and/or rectal pain, swelling, or bleeding; and reports of behavioral disturbances such as phobias, sudden irritability, regressive behavior, a decline in school performance, running away from home, drug abuse, excessive masturbation, and/or sexually precocious behavior and comments.

283. Thomas, J.N. and Rogers, C.M. "Sexual Abuse of Children: Case Finding and Clinical Assessment." **Nursing Clinics of North America,** 16(1): 179-181, March 1981.

Cases of child molestation are discovered in a medical setting by direct disclosure, by suspicions expressed by adults, and by assessment by medical personnel. Medical indicators of sexual molestation include: bruises, lacerations, abrasions, or erythema in the genital or rectal area; unexplained vaginal or rectal bleeding; urethral inflammation or inflammation of the inguinal lymph glands; pregnancy; and in boys, painful urination or penile swelling or discharge. Behavioral indicators include regressive behavior, phobias, running away from home, substance abuse, rapid personality change, and sex-related problems. Techniques for assessment, decision-making, and referral are also discussed.

284. White, S.; Loda, F.A.; Ingram, D.L.; and Pearson, A. "Sexually Transmitted Diseases in Sexually Abused Children." **Pediatrics,** 72(1): 16-21, July 1983.

A review of the cases of 409 children referred to a hospital program for suspected sexual molestation shows that 13% have sexually transmitted diseases including gonorrhea, syphillis, trichomon iasis, and condyloma acuminata. No attempts to diagnose herpes or chlamydia were made in this study.

285. Woodling, B.A. and Heger, A. "The Use of the Colposcope in the Diagnosis of Sexual Abuse in the Pediatric Age Group." **Child Abuse and Neglect,** 10(1): 111-114, 1986.

This study suggests that with the use of the colposcope which has a high magnification potential, the subtle findings of sexual abuse in children, such as abrasions, avulsions, contusions, ecchymoses, transections, focal edema, and petechiae can be discovered. It is concluded that the use of this instrument can increase the corroboration of visual findings to 85%.

Disclosure of Sexual Molestation

One of the more problematic areas in the intervention in cases of suspected sexual molestation is the child's reticence to disclose the incident. Delays in disclosure, inconsistencies, and retractions are commonly reported in the literature. The following references focus on the narrow issue of disclosure, discuss the problems with it, and posit some reasons why these difficulties exist.

286. Burgess, A.W. and Holmstrom, L.L. "Sexual Trauma of Children and Adolescents." **Nursing Clinics of North America,** 10(3): 551-563, September 1975.

Forty-two accessory to sex victims of child molestation were interviewed to discover the effects of the pressure for secrecy and the impact of the disclosure of the molestation on them. Clinical management of the child also is discussed.

287. Conte, J.R. and Berliner, L. "Sexual Abuse of Children: Implications for Practice." **Social Casework,** 62(10): 601-607, December 1981.

Only 16% of the 583 sexually molested children in this hospital referred sample reported the molestation to anyone within forty-eight hours of its occurrence.

288. Ferenczi, S. "Confusion of Tongues Between Adults and the Child." **International Journal of Psychoanalysis,** 30: 225-230, 1949.

Because of the overwhelming feelings of helplessness and anxiety produced by the sexual molestation experience, very young children often will experience confusion as to whether the molestation occurred in reality or in fantasy, and may deny that it was real when interviewed or questioned by an adult.

289. Gruber, K.J. "The Child Victim's Role in Sexual Assault by Adults." **Child Welfare,** 40(5): 305-311, May 1981.

Children often cooperate with adults who sexually approach them and then do not disclose the sexual molestation to others. The reasons for doing so may arise out of their fear of displeasing the adult; the promise of favors and gifts by the adult; their enjoyment of the attention and affection; and other situational pressures.

290. Rickarby, G.A. "Patterns of Sexual Abuse in Children." **Medical Journal of Australia**, 142(12): 636-637, June 10, 1985.

Two factors that complicate the child's disclosure of sexual molestation are discussed: the child's young age, and the child's fear of the molester and of the consequences of disclosure.

291. Rimsza, M.E. and Niggemann, E.H. "Medical Evaluation of Sexually Abused Children: A Review of 311 Cases." **Pediatrics**, 69(1): 8-14, January 1982.

Children's reticence to disclose incidents of molestation is reflected in this hospital sample of 311 sexually molested children. Only 45% of the sample was medically examined within three days of the incident; factors such as the fear of punishment, of not being believed, of being abandoned or rejected, as well as the secondary gains of gifts and favors are believed to underlie these delays in disclosure.

292. Rosenfeld, A.A.; Nadelson, C.C.; and Kreiger, M. "Incest and Sexual Abuse of Children." **Journal of the American Academy of Child Psychiatry**, 16: 327-339, 1977.

When an actual traumatic sexual molestation has occurred in childhood, it may be repressed, displaced, or substituted for a memory of a less traumatic event. The child's disclosure of the molestation, consequently, may be vague, inconsistent, or casually delivered.

293. Summit, R.C. "The Child Sexual Abuse Accommodation Syndrome." **Child Abuse and Neglect**, 7(2): 177-193, 1983.

The accommodation syndrome classifies the most typical reactions of a child to sexual molestation by describing the basic childhood vulnerabilities of accommodation and helplessness, and the child's reactions of secrecy, delayed and unconvincing disclosure, and retraction which are sequentially contingent upon sexual abuse.

294. Trankell, A. "Was Lars Sexually Assaulted? A Study in the Reliability of Witnesses and of Experts." **Journal of Abnormal and Social Psychology**, 56(3): 385-395, May 1958.

The case of Lars, a five year old boy who had accused an adult of coercing him into a single incident of sexual molestation, is presented. Although the boy's disclosure seemed credible at first, and although he could give substantial details as to the outlay of the alleged perpetrator's apartment, the psychiatrist who evaluated all parties concerned in this case finally concluded that Lars had been given the suggestion of sexual molestation by a young playmate and then had used it as an accusation to divert his mother's attention from other misbehavior in which he had been involved and for which she was reprimanding him.

Interviewing Children

Many factors complicate the process of interviewing sexually molested children. Their reticence to disclose, their developmentally based difficulties with language and concepts, and their post-molestation emotional reactions all interfere with the interviewing procedure. The following references examine these problems and suggest creative and innovative ways of circumventing them so that factual information about the nature of the molestation and the identity of the perpetrator can be ascertained.

295. Burgess, A.W.; McCausland, M.P.; and Wolbert, W.A. "Children's Drawings as Indicators of Sexual Trauma." **Perspectives in Psychiatric Care,** 19(2): 50-58, March/April 1981.

Drawings of a sexually molested child are used in conjunction with an interview to assess the degree of emotional trauma the child has experienced and to gauge the child's progress in resolving molestation-related issues in therapy.

296. Falk, G.J. "The Public Image of the Sex Offender." **Mental Hygiene,** 48(4): 612-620, October 1964.

Urban, middle class society has the most influence on the development of laws and proscribed punishments for breaking those laws, so stereotypes and myths it has about sexual offenders are particularly important to examine. Because of the hysteria about child molestation that is a feature of that segment of society, many men have been railroaded on sexual offense charges by spiteful children who have rehearsed their false accusations under prolonged questioning by police and/or mental health practitioners.

297. Faller, K.C. "Is the Child Victim of Sexual Abuse Telling the Truth?" **Child Abuse and Neglect,** 8(4): 473-481, 1984.

Based upon the study of 120 cases of child molestation, a procedure for assessing the truthfulness of a child's allegation of sexual abuse is offered. The procedure focuses on the nature of the disclosure; the child's account of the alleged molestation, including details regarding physical and emotional responses as well as the details about the pressure for secrecy; behavioral and emotional indicators of sexual abuse; and assessments of any pressures on the child to lie. Determining the child's accurate sexual knowledge and the names of body parts are necessary first steps in interviewing the alleged victim; anatomically correct dolls and unstructured play experiences can be useful adjuncts to the interviewing process.

298. Jones, J.G. "Sexual Abuse of Children: Current Concepts." **American Journal of Diseases of Children,** 136(2): 142-146, February 1982.

Guidelines for interviewing sexually molested children and for conducting medical examinations are discussed.

299. Jones, R.J.; Gruber, K.; and Freeman, M.H. "Reactions of Adolescents to Being Interviewed About Their Sexual Assault Experiences." **Journal of Sex Research,** 19(2): 160-172, May 1983.

As part of a youth protection survey, the reactions of a sample of adolescents to being explicitly and extensively interviewed about their personal sexual activities and their sexual assault histories are assessed. Sixty-nine adolescents, all currently or recently in residence in a delinquency treatment program, are interviewed and then asked questions regarding their level of comfort in responding to this survey. Not a great deal of discomfort is noted in the sharing of personal sexual activities; however those adolescents with histories of sexual molestation describe a great deal of discomfort in talking about those experiences.

300. Kelley, S.J. "Drawing: Critical Communications for Sexually Abused Children." **Pediatric Nursing,** 11(6): 421-426, November/December 1985.

The use of children's drawings to evaluate the sexual molestation experience and its impact on the child is described.

301. Miller, E.L. "Interviewing the Sexually Abused Child." **American Journal of Maternal/Child Nursing,** 10(2): 103-105, March/April 1985.

The successful interview with a sexually molested child depends upon first gaining the trust of the child. The interview should take place in a neutral setting and the child should be interviewed alone. Anatomically correct dolls and/or pictures can be helpful in the process. The child's language should be used by the interviewer, and the process should be carefully recorded.

302. Schuh, S.E. and Ralston, M.E. "Medical Interview of Sexually Abused Children." **Southern Medical Journal,** 78(3): 245-251, March 1985.

The role of the physician in conducting a medical interview with a sexually molested child is discussed. It is strongly advised that the physician be aware of his or her own blind spots and prejudices in this area and that care be taken not to blame the child for the molestation. The development of trust and communication with the child is essential for the medical examination which will follow.

303. Swann, A. "Therapeutic Dolls." **Nursing Mirror,** 161(17): 15, 18-20, October 23, 1985.

The use of anatomically correct dolls in interviewing and evaluating sexually molested children is described.

Psychological and Behavioral Effects

The experience of being sexually molested often has a negative impact on the emotional well-being and on the behavior of the child. The following references examine that impact and postulate psychological indicators of sexual molestation.

304. Adams-Tucker, C. "Proximate Effects of Sexual Abuse in Childhood: A Report on Twenty-Eight Children." **American Journal of Psychiatry,** 139(10): 1252-1256, October 1982.

The Louisville Behavior Checklist was administered to significant adults in the lives of 28 sexually molested children, who range in age from two to fifteen. Test results show that all of the children are symptomatic in one of the following areas: self-destructive, suicidal, and/or withdrawing behavior; sexual complaints, running away and/or aggressive behavior; peer, school, and/or parent problems; and anxiety, psychosomatic, and/or sleep related problems. The emotional disturbance experienced by the children is most severe when the sexual molestation begins at an early age and continues repetitively over a long period of time; or when it begins in the adolescent years, even though its frequency and duration may be limited. All of the subjects are experiencing emotional and behavioral problems as serious as those of children seeking psychiatric help for any reason.

305. Adams-Tucker, C. "Defense Mechanisms Used by Sexually Abused Children." **Children Today,** 14(1): 8-12, 34, January/February 1985.

The psychological defense mechanisms used by 26 sexually molested children, ages 2 to 15, were analyzed by reviewing their psychiatric records and by interviewing their therapists. Differences in the defensive style were also analyzed according to the variables of gender, age, severity of psychopathology, and the duration of the molestation. Narcissistic defenses, including denial, distortion, and delusional projection, were identified for 13 of the children; neurotic defenses such as sexualization, displacement, controlling, reaction formation, somatization, dissociation, and externalization were identified for 15 of the children. Immature defenses, including introjection, acting out, schizoid fantasies, passive-aggression, regression, blocking and hypochondriasis were identified for 25 of the children; and the remaining 5 children used mature defenses such as suppression and altruism. Males tend most often to use immature mechanisms, while females most often use neurotic and immature mechanisms. Young children have the fewest identifiable defense mechanisms, and school age children show the widest range of defenses. A wide range of defense mechanisms is used by severely disturbed children. No pattern related to the duration of the abuse could be found. Children molested by nonfamily persons tended most often to show defenses of acting out, denial, schizoid fantasies, and introjection, but those who received the quickest and most complete support from a caregiving adult tended to use fewer defense mechanisms.

306. Bender, L. and Blau, A. "The Reactions of Children to Sexual Relationships with Adults." **American Journal of Orthopsychiatry,** 7(4): 500-518, October 1937.

Less evidence of fear, anxiety, guilt, or psychic trauma than was expected is discovered in the reactions of children, ages five to twelve, who were sexually molested by adults. Eleven of these 16 children were molested by adults who were nonfamily persons. Most of the children exhibit either a frank, open attitude about the molestation, or are bold, flaunting, and even brazen about it. This observation leads to the conclusion that the children may have been the actual seducers, rather than those innocently seduced, and that the children's explanations that they were bribed, coerced, or forced into sexual acts by the adults are only rationalizations to explain away their own culpability. No negative effects of the molestation are found for 44% of the sample; regression to infantile behavior and fixation on genital preoccupations are found for 19% of the sample; and the remainder shows a variety of minor emotional and/or behavioral reactions. Those children who were sexually molested by family members tend to show more negative symptomatology than children who were molested by nonfamily persons.

307. Bender, L. and Grugett, A.E. "A Follow-Up Report on Children Who Had Atypical Sexual Experiences." **American Journal of Orthopsychiatry,** 22(4): 825-837, October 1952.

A followup of 14 sexually molested children conducted a decade after their referral to a psychiatric service shows that most have adjusted well in their late adolescence, a fact that is particularly true for those who had been removed from their homes and placed in alternative environments.

308. Brant, R.S.T. and Tisza, V.B. "The Sexually Misused Child." **American Journal of Orthopsychiatry,** 47(1): 80-90, January 1977.

This retrospective study of the hospital records of 52 sexually molested children finds that the following symptoms are commonly noted: reddened genitals, eating and sleeping disorders, and altered activity levels in molested infants. Because toddlers and young children have difficulty in verbally expressing their anxiety, physical and behavioral symptoms may be present. Those may include: genital irritation, discharge, or infection; psychosomatic complaints, especially of stomachaches and dysuria; venereal disease; and a wide range of behavioral problems that include enuresis, encopresis, hyperactivity, sleeping and eating disorders, compulsive behaviors, precocious sex play, excessive sexual curiosity, compulsive masturbation, deficits in attention, and separation anxiety.

309. Brooks, B. "Sexually Abused Children and Adolescent Identity Development." **American Journal of Psychotherapy,** 39(3): 401-410, July 1985.

Two conflicts are especially noted for female adolescents who were sexually molested as children but who had told no one until years later: an intrapsychic identification with bad objects, and an inhibition of the search for truth that is characteristic of the adolescent stage of development. This hypothesis is supported by the testing of 29 adolescent girls who are patients in a residential treatment center for emotionally disturbed adolescents.

Although only one of the girls has a documented history of sexual abuse that is in her record, the girls' responses to a battery of tests reveal that an additional 18 of the girls have a previously undiscovered history of sexual molestation. In addition, test results show that sexually molested girls tend to be more hostile, paranoid, and depressed, and have more psychotic concerns than do the other girls; despite that finding, a significant proportion of the molested girls deny that they have problems. It is hypothesized that denial is a defense against individual conflicts and an attempt to maintain an image of the intrapsychic world as good.

310. Chaneles, S. "Child Victims of Sexual Offenses." **Federal Probation,** 31(2): 52-56, June 1967.

Results of a study of children who have been sexually molested show that an immediate reaction of distrust of adults is predictable. Symptoms that may be noted include nightmares, withdrawal, aggression, and behavioral extremes.

311. DeVine, R. "Discovering and Treating Sexual Abuse of Children." **Medical Aspects of Human Sexuality,** 14(10): 25-26, October 1980.

Behavioral symptoms of molestation include: a reluctance to be with a particular person; disturbances in normal behavior patterns; more advanced sexual play activities; and an unusual interest in their parents' bodies. Physical symptoms include vaginal discharge or bleeding, or discomfort in the anal and/or genital area.

312. deYoung, M. "Counterphobic Behavior in Multiply Molested Children." **Child Welfare,** 63(4): 333-339, July/August 1984.

Four children who seemed to have encouraged their repeated sexual victimization are examined. Their "seductive" behavior is explained as being a symptom of counterphobia, the attempt to master the anxiety created by their initial sexual molestation by unconsciously and compulsively confronting the source of that anxiety by recreating victimizing situations.

313. Ellerstein, N.S. and Canacan, W. "Sexual Abuse of Boys." **American Journal of Diseases of Children,** 134(3): 255-257, March 1980.

A review of the hospital records of 16 boys who were sexually molested shows that all were molested by males and that in 87% of the cases, the offending adult was a nonfamily person. The mean age of the boys at the time of molestation was 9.7 years. Anal or perianal trauma is noted in the medical examinations of 44% of the boys.

314. Elonen, A.S. and Zwarensteyn, S.B. "Sexual Trauma in Young Blind Children." **New Outlook for the Blind,** 69(10): 440-442, December 1975.

A significant percentage of severely disturbed blind children referred for training have a childhood history of sexual molestation. Six case studies are presented to demonstrate the vulnerability of blind children to sexually victimizing behaviors by adults.

315. Fagan, J. and McMahon, P.P. "Incipient Multiple Personality in Children: Four Cases." **Journal of Nervous and Mental Disease,** 172(1): 26-36, January 1984.

This study describes four cases where dual identity and/or trance states were demonstrated by young children in response to inquiries or stimuli related to traumatic events; two of these children had been sexually molested. A list of twenty behavioral signs of incipient multiple personality in children is presented on the basis of these cases and a review of the literature. These indices include: trance states; responds to more than one name; marked changes in personality; peculiar forgetfulness; vague physical symptoms; inconsistent school work; disruptive behavior; symptoms and behaviors that perplex professionals; lies; is not affected by disclipline; a stoically indifferent or strong objection to discipline; delinquent behavior; self-injurious behavior; homicidal behavior; suicidal behavior; precocious sexuality; truancy; feelings of loneliness; physical complaints; and hysteric symptoms such as sleepwalking, seizures, paralysis, loss of sensation, or sudden blindness. Subjective experiences reported by the child that also may be indicative of incipient multiple personality include losses of time; hears voices inside his or her head; has imaginary playmates; is lonely; and is called by others by the wrong name. Family pathology that creates and/or sustains this pathology is discussed as are treatment strategies, including a systematic play therapy approach.

316. Finch, S.M. "Sexual Activity of Children with Other Children and Adults." **Clinical Pediatrics,** 6(1): 1-2, January 1967.

This brief review of children's sexual experimentation with peers, incest and child molestation emphasizes the polymorphous perversity of children which allows them to be easily led into a variety of sexual activities. The role that some children play in inviting and maintaining the sexual contact with an adult is also examined.

317. Finch, S.M. "Adult Seduction of the Child: Effects on the Child." **Medical Aspects of Human Sexuality,** 7(3): 170-185, March 1973.

It is not inevitable that sexually molested children will experience serious emotional problems. Children are polymorphous perverse; they have not achieved genital primacy and can find pleasure in many kinds of sexual stimulation. Children may play some role in setting up the molestation so guilt is a predictable post-molestation symptom. In general, the more violent and unexpected the act of molestation, the more emotional trauma the child is likely to experience.

318. Finkelhor, D. "The Sexual Abuse of Boys." **Victimology: An International Journal,** 6(1-4): 76-84, 1981.

Contrary to popular belief, young boys are sexually molested at a rate that although less than it is for girls, is still much higher than most people realize. They are most likely to be molested by male perpetrators, and more likely than girls to be molested by a nonfamily person. A pervasive double standard often hinders the recognition and the treatment of molested boys.

Both short and longerterm effects of the molestation of boys must be more carefully and thoroughly examined.

319. Finkelhor, D. and Browne, A. "The Traumatic Impact of Child Sexual Abuse: A Conceptualization." **American Journal of Orthopsychiatry,** 55(4): 530-541, October 1985.

A model that specifies how and why sexual abuse results in trauma is proposed. It postulates that the experience of sexual abuse can be analyzed in terms of four traumagenic dynamics that can alter the child's cognitive and emotional orientation to the world and to him/herself, and that can interfere with healthy coping. The first of these dynamics, traumatic sexualization, refers to the process in which the child's sexuality is shaped in developmentally inappropriate ways by the sexual abuse. This may result in such behavioral symptoms as sexual preoccupation, repetitive sexual behavior in play, repeated masturbation, and sexual aggressiveness. Remnants of that trauma may later create an aversion to sex, flashbacks to the molestation experience, and a variety of sexual dysfunctions as adults. Betrayal, the second dynamic, occurs when the child realizes that someone loved and trusted has caused him or her harm by the sexual abuse. Grief reactions, depression, and disillusionment may result from that realization, and adult problems centered around this dynamic may include relationship problems, impaired judgment, and antisocial behavior. The third dynamic, powerlessness, refers to the process in which the child's will and desires are constantly contravened by the sexual abuse, creating fear and anxiety which may show in nightmares, phobias, suicidal behavior, running away, and in adult years may manifest itself in attempts to regain power by becoming controlling, domineering, and aggressive. Finally, the dynamic of stigmatization occurs through the process of blaming the child for the abuse or in other ways adversely labeling the child. Guilt, shame, feelings of isolation, and low self-esteem may be the results of this dynamic and may persist into the adult years.

320. Gomes-Schwartz, B.; Horowitz, J.M.; and Sauzier, M. "Severity of Emotional Distress Among Sexually Abused Preschool, School-Age, and Adolescent Children." **Hospital and Community Psychiatry,** 36(5): 503-508, May 1985.

The Louisville Behavior Checklist was administered to 156 sexually molested children referred to a hospital treatment program, and their scores were compared to norms published for normal children and for psychologically disturbed children. Although sexually molested preschoolers show more behavioral disturbance than normal children, their scores on the test are lower than those of psychologically disturbed children. In every area except somatic complaints, sexually molested school age children show more psychopathology than normal children; the most common symptoms they demonstrate are anger, self-destructive behavior, internalized anxiety, and impulsivity. Sexually molested adolescents also show high test scores in the areas of anxiety, depression, and obsessive concerns. Test results show that in general, sexually molested children have more behavior problems and symptoms of emotional harm than normal children, but less than psychologically disturbed children.

321. Gross, M. "Incest and Hysterical Seizures." **Medical Hypoanalysis,** 3(4): 146-152, November 1982.

Six cases of hysterical seizures in adolescents, one of whom was sexually molested by a nonfamily person while the others were incestuously abused, are described in detail. The similarity of the seizure to the sexual act is hypothesized as the unconscious motivation behind the choice of this symptom. The seizures become a way for the unconscious mind to act out and abreact the sexual trauma, thereby relieving the ego of the tension associated with it.

322. Gruber, K.J. and Jones, Robert J. "Does Sexual Abuse Lead to Delinquent Behavior? A Critical Look at the Evidence." **Victimology: An International Journal,** 6(1-4): 85-91, 1981.

The literature has strongly suggested that there is a causal relationship between sexual molestation and later delinquent behavior on the part of the child, but there is little empirical evidence to support that contention. This study suggests two alternative explanations: that the socio-personal backgrounds of sexually molested children are very similar to that of delinquent children; and that by committing the delinquent act, the child puts himself or herself into situations in which the risk of sexual molestation is high. The study also develops a conceptual scheme regarding the determinants of sexual molestation.

323. Gruber, K.J. "The Child Victim's Role in Sexual Assault by Adults." **Child Welfare,** 40(5): 305-311, May 1981.

Children often cooperate with adults who sexually approach them and then do not disclose the sexual molestation to others. The reasons for doing so may arise out of their fear of displeasing the adult; the promise of favors and gifts by the adult; their enjoyment of the attention and affection; and other situational pressures.

324. Grunseit, F. "Sexual Abuse of Children: Issues, Views and Comments." **Medical Journal of Australia,** 142(12): 637-639, June 10, 1985.

A general overview of the dynamics of sexual molestation and its effects on children is presented.

325. Jones, R.J.; Gruber, K.; and Freeman, M.H. "Reactions of Adolescents to Being Interviewed About Their Sexual Assault Experiences." **Journal of Sex Research,** 19(2): 160-172, May 1983.

As part of a youth protection survey, the reactions of a sample of adolescents to being explicitly and extensively interviewed about their personal sexual activities and their sexual assault histories are assessed. Sixty-nine adolescents, all currently or recently in residence in a delinquency treatment program, are interviewed and then asked questions regarding their level of comfort in responding to this survey. Not a great deal of discomfort is noted in the sharing of personal sexual activities; however those adolescents with histories of sexual molestation describe a great deal of discomfort in talking about those experiences.

326. Kelley, S.J. "Learned Helplessness in the Sexually Abused Child." **Issues in Comprehensive Pediatric Nursing,** 9(3): 193-207, 1986.

A learned helplessness model is suggested to explain the behavior of children during and following the molestation.

327. Kempe, C.H. "Sexual Abuse, Another Hidden Pediatric Problem: The 1977 C. Anderson Aldrich Lecture." **Pediatrics,** 62(3): 382-389, September 1978.

Defining sexual abuse as the involvement of dependent, developmentally immature children in sexual activities they do not fully understand, to which they are unable to give informed consent, or that violate the taboos of family roles, the nature and extent of the problem are discussed. Physicians are advised to look for subtle clinical findings such as anxiety, fear, insomnia, conversion hysteria, weight gain or loss, and behavioral problems such as truancy, school failure, and running away as indicators of sexual molestation. They are also advised to believe children's disclosures of sexual molestation since experience shows that children do not fabricate stories of detailed sexual activity.

328. LaBarbera, J.D. and Dozier, E. "Hysterical Seizures: The Role of Sexual Exploitation." **Psychosomatics,** 21(11): 897-903, December 1980.

Four cases of hysterical seizures, three of which were precipitated by sexual molestation incidents with nonfamily persons, are described. Hysterical seizures can be prompted by sexually charged events for girls who exhibit ambivalence about sexual issues and sexual identity.

329. Mannarino, A.P. and Cohen, J.A. "A Clinical-Demographic Study of Sexually Abused Children." **Child Abuse and Neglect,** 10(1): 17-23, 1986.

The aim of this study is to provide clinical and demographic data on sexually molested children to challenge some of the widely held assumptions that appear in the literature. The subjects are 45 sexually molested children, ages three to sixteen; they come from all socioeconomic classes and 30% of them are Black. All of the children were given intelligence tests and results show a mean I.Q. of 92.9 points. The vast majority of the children experienced fondling; 11% experienced vaginal, oral, or rectal intercourse. Although none of the children had been physically forced into the act, 17% did report having been threatened by the molester. The parents of the children were asked to fill out a symptom checklist and 69% of the children display at least one symptom. Nightmares are most commonly reported; anxiety, clinging behavior, and feelings of sadness are also common; enuresis occurred for some of the children as did inappropriate sexual behaviors.

330. O'Neal, P.; Schaefer, J.; Bergman, J.; and Robins, L.N. "A Psychiatric Evaluation of Adults Who Had Sexual Problems as Children: A Thirty Year Follow-Up Study." **Human Organization,** 19(1): 32-39, Spring 1960.

The adult adjustment of people with childhood histories of sexual problems who were treated at a child guidance clinic is compared to that of people who were treated as children for other types of problems. "Sexual problems" are defined as sexual activities in conflict with society's norms, for the purposes of this study. The comparison shows that a significant proportion of those subjects who had exhibited sexual problems as children had been sexually molested before going into treatment and that they showed a variety of antisocial behavior such as lying, stealing, running away, and school problems while they were in treatment. As adults, this group has a higher divorce rate and a higher rate of antisocial sexual behavior such as promiscuity, prostitution, and extramarital affairs than does the control group. They do not, however, show more emotional disturbance.

331. Paperny, D.M. and Deisher, R.W. "Maltreatment of Adolescents: The Relationship to a Predisposition Toward Violent Behavior and Delinquency." **Adolescence,** 18(71): 499-506, Fall 1983.

Interviews of 21 adolescent male prostitutes reveal that 43% were sexually molested before becoming prostitutes and that the majority of these molestation experiences were violent in nature. Physical abuse is documented in the backgrounds of 28% of these young men. It is theorized that an early history of physical and/or sexual abuse may lead to delinquency by diminishing the ability of the adolescent to cope with stress and by creating low self-esteem.

332. Rosenfeld, A.A. "The Clinical Management of Incest and Sexual Abuse in Children." **Journal of the American Medical Association,** 242(16): 1761-1764, October 1979.

Clues to the sexual molestation of children include genital complaints, sexually transmitted diseases, and reports of compulsive masturbation, sexual acting out, and any unpredictable and extreme alterations in behavior.

333. Ruch, L.O. and Chandler, S. M. "The Crisis Impact of Sexual Assault on Three Victim Groups: Adult Rape Victims, Child Rape Victims, and Incest Victims." **Journal of Social Service Research,** 5(1-2): 83-100, 1982.

The impact of sexual assault as measured by a standardized assessment scale is determined for a group of 283 adult rape victims, 78 child rape victims, and 47 child incest victims. Data reveal that child rape victims experience significantly less trauma than do incest victims. Any victim's trauma level will be high if verbal threats, physical force, the use of a weapon, victim resistance, or injuries to the victims are features of the sexual assault.

334. Sandfort, T.G. "Sex in Pedophiliac Relationships: An Empirical Investigation Among a Nonrepresentative Group of Boys." **Journal of Sex Research,** 20(2): 123-142, May 1984.

Twenty-five boys who have on-going, mutually agreed upon sexual relationships with adult males who are members of a Pedophile Workgroup in the Netherlands, participated in a structured interview which utilizes a Self-Confrontation Method that determines what is important for the person at a certain moment in his life and gives insight into the meaning of these events and feelings. All of the boys indicate a positive reaction to their sexual relationship with the pedophile and all believe that the relationship has a beneficial impact on their well-being. Although concerns about being discovered and punished did surface in the interviews, all of the boys stated that the pedophiles' attention to them, their respect for their feelings, and their friendship far outweighed the disadvantages of having such a relationship.

335. Schultz, L.G. and Jones, P. "Sexual Abuse of Children: Issues for Social Service and Health Professionals." **Child Welfare,** 62(2): 99-108, March/April 1983.

Indicators of sexual molestation in young children include nightmares, running away, poor peer relations, disruptive or aggressive behaviors, sexual self-consciousness, arriving early for school and leaving late, allegations of sexual mistreatment by siblings, and role reversal with the mother.

336. Silbert, M.H. "Sexual Child Abuse as an Antecedent to Prostitution." **Child Abuse and Neglect,** 5: 407-411, 1981.

A childhood history of sexual molestation is found in the backgrounds of 60% of the 200 adolescent and adult female street prostitutes who were interviewed in this study. The possible relationship between these early sexually coercive experiences and later prostitution is examined.

337. Silbert, M.H. and Pines, A.M. "Early Sexual Exploitation as an Influence in Prostitution." **Social Work,** 28(4): 285-289, July/August 1983.

Interviews with 200 juvenile and adult female prostitutes who work the streets of San Francisco reveal that 60% of them had been sexually molested as children or as adolescents, slightly less than half of them by a nonfamily person. Most rated the experience as very negative in its impact, although less than half of them ever told anyone about the incident. The possible relationship between early sexual molestation and prostitution is examined, and intervention strategies are proposed.

338. Thomas, J.N. "Yes, You Can Help a Sexually Abused Child." **RN,** 43(8): 23-29, August 1980.

On the basis of the medical examinations of 500 sexually molested children, 300 of whom were molested by a nonfamily person, the following symptoms are most commonly noted: sexually transmitted diseases; vaginal and/or rectal pain, swelling, or bleeding; and reports of behavioral disturbances such as phobias, sudden irritability, regressive behavior, a decline in school performance, running away from home, drug abuse, excessive masturbation, and/or sexually precocious behavior and comments.

339. Tsai, M. and Wagner, N.N. "Incest and Molestation: Problems of Childhood Sexuality." **Medical Times,** 109(7): 16-22, July 1981.

This general review of incest and child molestation emphasizes the immediate traumatic reaction the child is likely to have to the sexual contact with the adult. Symptoms of that reaction include sleep disorders, night terrors and nightmares, withdrawal, and hostility.

340. Weiss, J.; Rogers, E.; Darwin, M.; and Dutton, C. "A Study of Girl Sex Victims." **Psychiatric Quarterly**, 29(1): 1-27, January 1955.
Interviews and psychological testing of 72 sexually molested young girls suggest that there may be two categories of victims in cases of sexual molestation. Accidental victims tend to very young and to have been molested by a stranger in a single incident; they tend to disclose the incident to a trusted adult immediately after its occurrence. Participant victims, on the other hand, are usually attractive and appealing, and may have behaved seductively, thereby enticing the adult into the sexual act. They are usually involved in multiple sexual incidents over time and do not disclose these incidents to anyone. The mother of the child may play a collusive role in the sexual molestation since she often feels jealous of her daughter and has conflicts about the child's developing sexuality.

Effects of Childhood Molestation On Adults

The literature also investigates the longterm effects of a childhood history of sexual molestation on the adult. The following references examine the sequelae of molestation.

341. Carmen, E.H.; Rieker, P.P.; and Mills, T. "Victims of Violence and Psychiatric Illness." **American Journal of Psychiatry**, 141(3): 378-383, March 1984.
A childhood history of sexual molestation is discovered for 80 of the 188 adolescents and adults released from inpatient care at a mental hospital. When compared to patients without this history, this group stayed an average of 15 days longer in the mental hospital, and posed greater management and treatment problems because of poor self-esteem and unhealthy and/or self-destructive expressions of anger.

342. Finkelhor, D. and Browne, A. "The Traumatic Impact of Child Sexual Abuse: A Conceptualization." **American Journal of Orthopsychiatry**, 55(4): 530-541, October 1985.
A model that specifies how and why sexual abuse results in trauma is proposed. It postulates that the experience of sexual abuse can be analyzed in terms of four traumagenic dynamics that can alter the child's cognitive and emotional orientation to the world and to him/herself, and that can interfere with healthy coping. The first of these dynamics, traumatic sexualization, refers to the process in which the child's sexuality is shaped in developmentally inappropriate ways by the sexual abuse. This may result in such behavioral symptoms as sexual preoccupation, repetitive sexual behavior in play, repeated masturbation, and sexual aggressiveness. Remnants of

that trauma may later create an aversion to sex, flashbacks to the molestation experience, and a variety of sexual dysfunctions as adults. Betrayal, the second dynamic, occurs when the child realizes that someone loved and trusted has caused him or her harm by the sexual abuse. Grief reactions, depression, and disillusionment may result from that realization, and adult problems centered around this dynamic may include relationship problems, impaired judgment, and antisocial behavior. The third dynamic, powerlessness, refers to the process in which the child's will and desires are constantly contravened by the sexual abuse, creating fear and anxiety which may show in nightmares, phobias, suicidal behavior, running away, and in adult years may manifest itself in attempts to regain power by becoming controlling, domineering, and aggressive. Finally, the dynamic of stigmatization occurs through the process of blaming the child for the abuse or in other ways adversely labeling the child. Guilt, shame, feelings of isolation, and low self-esteem may be the results of this dynamic and may persist into the adult years.

343. Fritz, G.S.; Stoll, K.; and Wagner, N.N. "A Comparison of Males and Females Who were Sexually Molested as Children." **Journal of Sex and Marital Therapy**, 7(1): 54-59, Spring 1981.

Those female college students who stated on a questionnaire that they had had sexual molestation experiences as children are more than two times more likely than nonmolested females to also report current problems with sexual adjustment.

344. Fromuth, M.E. "The Relationship of Childhood Sexual Abuse with Later Psychological and Sexual Adjustment in a Sample of College Women." **Child Abuse and Neglect**, 10(1): 5-15, 1986.

The purpose of this study is to explore the relationship between sexual abuse and later psychological and sexual adjustments of a nonclinical sample of 383 female college students who completed a sexual history questionnaire, a Parental Support Scale, a Locus of Control Scale, the Beck Depression Inventory, the Hopkins Symptom Checklist, the Rosenberg Self-Esteem Scale, and the Sexual Self-Esteem Scale. The psychological test results of the 106 women who reported a childhood history of sexual molestation are not significantly different from those of the women who do not report a history of sexual molestation. Results of the tests measuring sexual adjustment suggest that a childhood history of sexual abuse may be related to an increased vulnerability to rape or other types of nonconsensual sexual behavior during the childhood and adolescent years, and to a wider range of sexual behavior and an increase in sexual activity. No evidence of a relationship between childhood sexual abuse and later sexual problems or the development of a pattern of sex avoidance is discovered.

345. Katan, A. "Children Who Were Raped." **Psychoanalytic Study of the Child**, 28: 208-224, 1973.

Women who were raped as children frequently have low self-esteem as adults and tend to identify with men so that they become aggressive in an attempt to compensate for their feelings of worthlessness. Fixated at the anal-sadistic stage, the aggressive drive never becomes tempered with tender, warm, and affectionate feelings.

346. Kilpatrick, A.C. "Some Correlates of Women's Childhood Sexual Experiences: A Retrospective Study." **Journal of Sex Research**, 22(2): 221-242, May 1986.

A sample of 501 women, ages eighteen to sixty, was given a questionnaire requesting information on demographic, adult functioning, and sexual history variables. Sexual experiences that range in seriousness from fondling to intercourse during childhood are reported by 55% of the women. Adult functioning scores of women reporting childhood sexual experiences are not significantly different from those who do not; however, when the sexual experience is described as abusive, guilt-provoking, harmful or pressured, and the partner in that experience was a parent or relative, a significantly more negative impact on adult functioning is noted.

347. Lister, E.D. "Forced Silence: A Neglected Dimension of Trauma." **American Journal of Psychiatry,** 139(7): 872-876, July 1982.

The demand the victim remain silent is one overlooked aspect of a traumatic experience. This study examines the dimensions of forced secrecy through the presentation of two cases of masochistic women in therapy. One had been repeatedly sexually molested as a child and had a variety of self-destructive relationships with men; the other had been physically abused by her mother and also had had a series of destructive relationships with men. The bond of fear between the perpetrator of the original abuse causes identification with the aggressor, and that, coupled with the child's vulnerability, the fear of repetition, and a pattern of self-protective compliance create a fertile ground for the learning of masochistic behavior which may persist into adulthood. The difficulties in therapy with these kinds of clients are also discussed.

348. Mills, T.; Rieker, P.P.; and Carmen, E.H. "Hospitalization Experiences of Victims of Abuse." **Victimology: An International Journal,** 9(3-4): 436-449, 1984.

A history of sexual molestation is discovered in the childhoods of 80 of 188 adolescents and adults released from inpatient care at a mental hospital; molestation was strongly suspected but not confirmed for an additional 13 ex-patients. A record review shows that mental patients with a history of sexual molestation tend to have had longer hospital stays and present management and treatment problems while hospitalized.

349. O'Neal, P.; Schaefer, J.; Bergman, J.; and Robins, L.N. "A Psychiatric Evaluation of Adults Who Had Sexual Problems as Children: A Thirty Year Follow-Up Study." **Human Organization**, 19(1): 32-39, Spring 1960.

The adult adjustment of people with childhood histories of sexual problems who were treated at a child guidance clinic is compared to that of people who were treated as children for other types of problems. "Sexual problems" are defined as sexual activities in conflict with society's norms, for the purposes of this study. The comparison shows that a significant proportion of those subjects who had exhibited sexual problems as children had been sexually molested before going into treatment and that they showed a variety of antisocial behavior such as lying, stealing, running away, and school problems while they were in treatment. As adults, this group has a higher divorce rate and a higher rate of antisocial sexual behavior such as promiscuity, prostitution, and extramarital affairs than does the control group. They do not, however, show more emotional disturbance.

350. Petrovich, M. and Templer, D.I. "Heterosexual Molestation of Children Who Later Became Rapists." **Psychological Reports,** 54(3): 810, June 1984.

A childhood history of sexual molestation by a female is found in the backgrounds of 59% of the 83 incarcerated adult male rapists in this study. Their ages at the time of the molestation ranged from four to sixteen years; most had experienced sexual intercourse on repeated occasions with an older female who was not related to them. Speculations as to what kind of a relationship these childhood experiences may have had on their adult sexually aggressive behavior with women are presented.

351. Roland, B.C.; Zelhart, P.F.; and Cochran, S.W. "MMPI Correlates of Clinical Women Who Report Early Sexual Abuse." **Journal of Clinical Psychology,** 41(6): 763-766, November 1985.

The MMPI scores of 26 women in psychotherapy who had reported a childhood history of sexual molestation were compared to the scores of 25 women in therapy who had not been molested as children. Results show that when validity, K-corrected subscales and demographic data for each subject are submitted to a stepwise mutivariate discriminant analysis, a linear function of the Hy (Hysteria), MF (Masculinity/Femininity), Hs (Hypochondriasis), and Pd (Psychopathic Deviate) scales will correctly identify women with a history of childhood molestation 73% of the time.

352. Silbert, M.H. "Prostitution and Sexual Assault: Summary of Results." **International Journal for Biosocial Research,** 3(2): 69-71, 1982.

Interviews with 200 juvenile and adult female prostitutes reveal that 60% of them had been sexually molested as children or as adolescents, and that most who had, had run away from home to escape the sexual abuse and then had started prostituting as a means of economic survival. Once on the streets, those prostitutes with a history of sexual molestation in their childhood tend to be repeatedly victimized by other prostitutes, pimps, and by their customers.

353. Silbert, M.H. and Pines, A.M. "Early Sexual Exploitation as an Influence in Prostitution." **Social Work,** 28(4): 285-289, July/August 1983.

Interviews with 200 juvenile and adult female prostitutes who work the streets of San Francisco reveal that 60% of them had been sexually molested as children or as adolescents, slightly less than half of them by a nonfamily person. Most rated the experience as very negative in its impact, although less than half of them ever told anyone about the incident. The possible relationship between early sexual molestation and prostitution is examined, and intervention strategies are proposed.

354. Tindall, R.H. "The Male Adolescent Involved with a Pederast Becomes an Adult." **Journal of Homosexuality,** 3(4): 373-387, Summer 1978.

This study looks at 9 adult males, each of whom had had a longterm sexual relationship with an older man when they were adolescents. As adults, none appears to have been emotionally traumatized by this kind of sexual relationship, and although a few of the men admit to homosexual fantasies and to some homosexual behavior as adults, none identifies himself as a homosexual. It is theorized that the lack of trauma and deleterious effects may be due to the fact that these had been consenting, non-coercive sexual relationships with men who were described as "fatherly" and with whom the adolescents had developed close friendships.

355. Tsai, M. and Wagner, N.N. "Therapy Groups for Women Sexually Molested as Children." **Archives of Sexual Behavior,** 7(5): 417-427, September 1978.

Prevalent clinical issues in adult females who have a childhood history of sexual molestation include guilt, depression, sexual dysfunction, and repetition compulsion.

356. Tsai, M. and Wagner, N.N. "Women Who Were Sexually Molested as Children." **Medical Aspects of Human Sexuality,** 13(8): 55-56, August 1979.

Problems commonly seen by physicians in adult women who had been sexually molested as children include guilt feelings, depression, a negative self-image, feelings of isolation, mistrust of men, and sexual dysfunction.

CHAPTER 7:
TREATMENT OF CHILD MOLESTERS

The treatment of child molesters has a long and controversial history. Most of the techniques referred to in the literature are behavioral in nature, and most boast positive results. The ethical dimension of some of these techniques, however, is frequently questioned, and the emphasis on psychotherapy as a viable approach to treatment only recently has been examined.

Covert Sensitization

One of the most consistently used treatment approaches with child molesters is covert sensitization. With this technique, the subject's sexual arousal to some stimulus involving children is paired with a noxious stimulus, such as an electrical shock or a foul odor. The goal of the treatment is to create within the subject's mind an association of his arousal to children with a punishment; in order to avoid the punishment, then, he avoids becoming sexually aroused to children.

357. Barlow, D.H.; Leitenberg, H.; and Agras, W.S. "Experimental Control of Sexual Deviation Through Manipulation of the Noxious Scene in Covert Sensitization." **Journal of Abnormal Psychology,** 74(5): 596-601, October 1969.
   A twenty-five year old male with a thirteen year history of child molestation participated in treatment during which descriptions of extremely noxious scenes were paired with sexually arousing scenes with children as the sexual object. This technique of covert sensitization is successful in decreasing the subject's deviant sexual behavior.

358. Brownell, K.D.; Hayes, S.C.; and Barlow, D.H. "Patterns of Appropriate and Deviant Sexual Arousal: The Behavioral Treatment of Multiple Sexual Deviations." **Journal of Consulting and Clinical Psychology,** 45(6): 1144-1155, December 1977.
   Five males, each exhibiting two patterns of deviant sexual arousal, in-

cluding child molestation, experience significant reductions in these patterns after completing a treatment program of covert sensitization.

359. Callahan, E.J. and Leitenberg, H. "Aversion Therapy for Sexual Deviation: Contingent Shock and Covert Sensitization." **Journal of Abnormal Psychology,** 81(1): 60-73, February 1973.

No significant differences are found in the results of using contingent shock versus using covert sensitization in the treatment of sexually deviant males, two of whom are child molesters.

360. Forgione, A.G. "The Use of Mannequins in the Behavioral Assessment of Child Molesters: Two Case Reports." **Behavior Therapy,** 7(5): 678-685, October 1976.

Two child molesters were asked to act out their reported behaviors with life sized mannequins while being photographed by an evaluator. The mannequins are found to elicit sexual responses from the men and to initiate a chain of behaviors that shows how the children are approached and treated. Details that are not part of the molesters' official records and which they do not volunteer to share with the evaluator become obvious with this approach. The photographs are then used as stimuli for aversive conditioning therapy with the molesters at a later date.

361. Hallam, R.S. and Rachman, S. "Some Effects of Aversion Therapy on Patients with Sexual Disorders." **Behavior Research and Therapy,** 10(1): 171-180, February 1972.

Seven sexually deviant males, two of whom are child molesters, are successfully treated with a course of electric shock aversion therapy.

362. Josiassen, R.C.; Fantuzzo, J.; and Rosen, A.C. "Treatment of Pedophilia Using Multistage Aversion Therapy and Social Skills Training." **Journal of Behavior Therapy and Experimental Psychiatry,** 11(1): 55-61, March 1980.

Using a 40-point scale of sexual arousal, a chronic child molester is asked to rate 678 slides variously depicting sexual behavior with children and with adult women. A multistage aversion therapy program is then used to change his behavior and fantasies. The first stage pairs electric shocks with slides of children; in the second stage the subject is helped with relaxation exercises after viewing slides of adult women; and in the third stage, shocks are given if his eyes scan or probe the slides of children. During each stage, heterosexual social skills training is also provided. Results of the treatment suggest that this multistage approach can be successful in reducing pedophilic behavior and fantasies.

363. Keltner, A.A. "The Control of Penile Tumescence with Biofeedback in Two Cases of Pedophilia." **Corrective and Social Psychiatry and Journal of Behavioral Techniques, Methods and Therapy,** 23(4): 117-121, 1977.

Using response-contingent conditioning in which verbal instructions and different reinforcements are made contingent upon the reduction of penile tumescence in response to slides depicting nude children, one child molester reports a significant change in behavior, mood, and self-esteem, and a significant reduction in pedophilic fantasies. The second child molester treated in this manner shows only a slight reduction in sexual arousal to sexual stimuli involving children.

364. Levin, S.M.; ˑ ry, S.M.; Gambaro, S.; Wofinsohn, L.; and Smith, A. "Case Studies: Variaˑions of Covert Sensitization in the Treatment of Pedophilic Behavior." **Journal of Consulting and Clinical Psychology,** 45(5): 896-907, October 1977.

Covert sensitization, using psychological as well as physical stimuli, is used to treat a 39 year old chronic child molester. Post-treatment MMPI results show a significant decrease in the D (Depression) scale and in the Si (Social Introversion) scale; lesser decreases are also noted in the Sc (Schizophrenia) scale and the Pd (Psychopathic Deviate) scale. Responses on the Sexual Interest Rating Scale show a significant decrease in sexual responses to young girls and an increase in sexual responsiveness to adult women. The changes persist at the ten month followup session.

365. Maletzky, B.M. "Self-Referred Versus Court-Referred Sexually Deviant Patients: Success with Assisted Covert Sensitization." **Behavior Therapy,** 11(3): 306-314, June 1980.

A group of self-referred child molesters and exhibitionists is treated with a covert sensitization technique in which an aversive odor is paired with scenes of sexually deviant behavior. The results are compared to those of a group of court-referred subjects. The data show that both groups experience a significant decrease in their phallometric responses to sexually deviant stimuli, and both groups report a marked decrease in their sexually deviant behavior. Followups at six, twelve, eighteen, twenty-four and thirty month intervals show a small but similar rate of recidivism within both groups. The data are striking for their lack of significant differences and can be interpreted to show that covert sensitization techniques can be successfully used with both court and self-referred subjects.

366. Marshall, W.L. and McKnight, R.D. "An Integrated Treatment Program for Sexual Offenders." **Canadian Psychiatric Association Journal,** 20(2): 133-138, March 1975.

Three incarcerated child molesters were treated by pairing electrical shocks with slides of children and then terminating the shocks with slides of adults, by training in social skills, and exposure to social interaction with staff on the ward and in the occupational therapy program. One subject was released and molested another child eighteen months later; one was released and has not recidivated after eight months; and the third is still incarcerated.

367. Quinsey, V.L.; Bergersen, S.G.; and Steinman, C.M. "Changes in Physiological and Verbal Responses of Child Molesters During Aversion Therapy." **Canadian Journal of Behavioral Science,** 8(2): 202-212, April 1976.

The skin conductance and phallometric measures of ten hospitalized child molesters are measured while they look at slides of adults and of children. Electric shocks are administered when there is a physiological response to a slide that has been identified as sexually stimulating by the subjects who previously had rated each slide according to a semantic differential scale. Results show that a combination of the phallometric and skin conductance techniques is useful in assessing changes in sexual preference over time, and that the pre- and post-test semantic differential and slide ranking exercises show an increase in sexual preferences for adults as opposed to children.

368. Rosenthall, T.L. "Response-Contingent Versus Fixed Punishment in Aversion Conditioning of Pedophilia: A Case Study." **Journal of Nervous and Mental Disease,** 156(6): 440-443, June 1973.

A response-contingent, or shaping, paradigm of aversive conditioning is used with a 31 year old chronic child molester who is also mildly mentally retarded. Pictures of a child which previously he had rated as sexually stimulating were shown to him, and when he verbally indicated that he was feeling sexually aroused, an electric shock was administered. No significant changes in his responses were noted, even when the intensity of the shock was increased, so a shaping paradigm was initiated in which the duration of the shock was varied as a function of the latency of his sexual arousal response to the stimuli. Dramatically positive results are found with this procedure, and the reduction in sexual responses to children persist at the thirty-two month followup session.

369. Serber, M. "Shame Aversion Therapy." **Journal of Behavior Therapy and Experimental Psychiatry,** 1(3): 213-215, September 1970.

Shame aversion therapy involves the recreation of the deviant sexual behavior in front of other people and in front of a mirror; theoretically, the shame reaction this produces will be habituated and stop the behavior. The technique is successfully used with a child molester, although for ethical reasons, a young adult female was substituted for a child in the therapy.

Biofeedback Treatment Techniques

Biofeedback techniques have shown some promise in the treatment of child molesters. The degree of conscious control over sexual arousal that these techniques teach a subject are shown to be helpful in reducing arousal to children.

370. Laws, D.R. "Treatment of Bisexual Pedophilia by a Biofeedback Assisted Self-Control Procedure." **Behavior Research and Therapy,** 18(3): 207-211, 1980.

A 24 year old bisexual child molester who had molested over a thousand young boys and who has persistent sexual fantasies about young girls was treated for 88 days with a biofeedback procedure which displays his erection response to sexually deviant stimuli. By using biofeedback techniques, he was able to exert conscious control over his sexual arousal responses to the deviant stimuli.

371. Quinsey, V.L.; Chaplin, T.C.; and Carrigan, W.F. "Biofeedback and Signaled Punishment in the Modification of Inappropriate Sexual Age Preferences." **Behavior Therapy,** 11(4): 567-576, September 1980.

The post-treatment phallometric responses of 30 child molesters who had received biofeedback therapy before their release from an institution are measured in this followup study. The post-treatment sex/age preferences are compared to those documented in their official records. Results show that after an average of two years in the community, the child molesters still phallometrically respond to slides of children; record reviews show that six of them had committed new offenses against children since their release. In part two of this study, 18 hospitalized child molesters received either biofeedback alone or in combination with signaled punishment aversion therapy in which a mild shock is administered when a colored light indicates that the phallometric response to a slide is above a preset limit. This combination approach is found to be more effective than biofeedback alone in altering the sex/age preferences of child molesters.

Orgasmic Reconditioning

The treatment technique of orgasmic reconditioning involves changing the molester's masturbatory fantasies from those of children to those of adults. It is theorized that once the subject begins to associate the pleasure of orgasm with sexual behavior with an adult, his arousal to children will be extinguished.

372. Foote, W.E. and Laws, D.R. "A Daily Alternation Procedure for Orgasmic Reconditioning with a Pedophile." **Journal of Behavior Therapy and Experimental Psychiatry,** 12(3): 267-273, September 1981.

A 38 year old hospitalized male with a long history of bisexual child molesting is successfully treated by a procedure which daily alternates masturbating to slides depicting nude children with those depicting nude adult women.

373. Kremsdorf, R.B.; Holmen, M.L.; and Laws, D.R. "Orgasmic Reconditioning with Deviant Imagery: A Case Report with a Pedophile." **Behavior Research and Therapy,** 18(3): 203-207, 1980.

A modified form of orgasmic reconditioning in which a child molester masturbates to nondeviant fantasies produces a significant reduction in his deviant sexual fantasies.

374. Marshall, W.L. "The Modification of Sexual Fantasies: A Combination Treatment Approach to the Reduction of Deviant Sexual Behavior." **Behavior Research and Therapy**, 11(4): 557-564, November 1973.

It is hypothesized that a combined aversion therapy/orgasmic reconditioning treatment program will reduce the attractiveness of deviant fantasies in a group of 12 sexual offenders which includes five child molesters. The subjects are instructed to use deviant fantasies to initiate masturbation and to continue with them until just before ejaculation and then switch to sexually appropriate fantasies. This procedure is continued until the subjects can control the fantasy content at ejaculation. The subjects are then asked to keep moving back to appropriate fantasies during the process of masturbation until they serve as initiating stimuli. This combined technique is successful in reducing the deviant sexual fantasies, increasing the appropriate ones, and changing behavior and attitudes.

375. VanDeventer, A.D. and Laws, D.R. "Orgasmic Reconditioning to Redirect Sexual Arousal in Pedophiles." **Behavior Therapy**, 9(5): 748-765, November 1978.

Two incarcerated homosexual child molesters were treated with orgasmic reconditioning techniques over an eight week period. Each was instructed to masturbate while saying his fantasies aloud, and the weeks each masturbated to a deviant theme were alternated with weeks of masturbation to an appropriate theme. After each session, phallometric measures were taken to stimuli of deviant and nondeviant material depicted in slides. Results show that one of the subjects demonstrates a significant reduction in his arousal to children while the other shows no changes.

Operant Conditioning

376. Wong, S.; Gaydos, G.R.; and Fuqua, R.W. "Operant Control of Pedophilia." **Behavior Modification**, 6(1): 73-84, January 1982.

The treatment of a mildly mentally retarded child molester is described. The subject, a resident in a group home, was observed in his neighborhood walks and any approaches to children were noted. Through the use of roleplays, the group home staff explained a no-approach philosophy and instituted restrictions and confinement for noncompliance. Significant decreases in approach behavior to children are noted as a result of this operant control approach.

Satiation Therapy

Satiation therapy involves the technique of prolonged masturbation to sexual fantasies involving children. It is hypothesized that the repeated exposure to these fantasies over time will eventually diminish their ability to produce sexual arousal.

377. Marshall, W.L. "Satiation Therapy: A Procedure for Reducing Deviant Sexual Arousal." **Journal of Applied Behavior Analysis,** 12(3): 377-389, Fall 1979.

Satiation therapy, the pairing of prolonged masturbation with verbalizations by the subject of his deviant sexual fantasies, is used to treat two chronic child molesters. In both cases, the treatment reduces deviant sexual interests. It appears that repeated exposure to deviant fantasies may exhaust the capacity of the subject to respond to them; with this technique that makes fantasies explicit by verbalizing them, their vagueness and their taboo both are removed, and that may reduce their attractiveness.

378. Marshall, W.L. and Barbaree, H.E. "The Reduction of Deviant Arousal: Satiation Treatment for Sexual Aggressors." **Criminal Justice and Behavior,** 5(4): 294-303, December 1978.

Since sexual offenders show the greatest sexual arousal to deviant sex, treatment should focus on decreasing heterosexual anxiety, increasing self-confidence and social competence, and controlling hostility and aggression. To accomplish these goals, the subject is instructed to verbalize his sexually deviant fantasies while he masturbates and to continue doing so after he ejaculates. This process of satiation associates boredom with the subject's sexual fantasies and motivates the person to modify his fantasies in order to maintain their capacity to arouse him.

Biosyntonic Treatment

379. Nolan, J.D. and Sandman, C. "'Biosyntonic' Therapy: Modification of an Operant Conditioning Approach to Pedophilia." **Journal of Consulting and Clinical Psychology,** 46(5): 1133-1140, October 1978.

Biosyntonic therapy assumes that there is an intimate relationship between attitudes, emotions, and the physiologic state of the person. A 32 year old child molester is shown a series of slides while his heart rate, respiration, skin potential, and peripheral vasomotor activity are being monitored. When his heart rate increases in response to a slide, he is given an electric shock; he is also given monetary rewards for voluntarily increasing his heart rate in response to slides of adults and for inhibiting it in response to slides of children. A significant decrease in his sexually deviant attitudes and behaviors is noted, suggesting both that the subject learned some voluntary control over his physiologic state, and that that control brought about changes in related emotions and attitudes.

In Vivo Treatment

380. Kohlenberg, R.J. "Treatment of a Homosexual Pedophiliac Using In Vivo Desensitization: A Case Study." **Journal of Abnormal Psychology,** 83(2): 192-195, April 1974.

A homosexual child molester is treated by pairing electric shocks with pictures of nude boys; once arousal to this stimulus is reduced, the subject is encouraged to actually engage in a graded sequence of sexual interactions with an adult male. This *in vivo* desensitization produces a significant change in the subject's behavior; he is sexually aroused by the adult male and has significantly reduced his sexual behavior with and sexual fantasies about young boys.

Automated Fading Treatment

381. Laws, D.R. and Pawlowski, A.V. "An Automated Fading Procedure to Alter Sexual Responsiveness in Pedophiles." **Journal of Homosexuality,** 1(2): 149-163, Winter 1974.

A nonadversive fading technique is used in the treatment of an incarcerated heterosexual child molester and an incarcerated homosexual child molester. Slides of children and of adults are superimposed and when the subjects produce an erection response above a designated criterion, the slide of the child fades out and the slide of the adult fades in; if the phallometric response then falls below the criterion, the fading procedure is reversed. Results show success in strengthening the sexual responses to the adult stimuli, although it is unclear as to whether the fading technique or the covert instructions the subjects gave themselves during the process is responsible for the positive changes.

Drug Therapy

An important and controversial avenue for the treatment of child molesters is drug therapy. Through the use of antiandrogen drugs, particularly Depo-Provera, the subject's sexual arousal in general is diminished; that, in turn, is believed to afford him more control over his behavior and to render him more amenable to psychotherapy. Unpleasant side effects of these types of drugs also must be anticipated, as the following references suggest.

382. Berlin, F. S. and Meinecke, C.F. "Treatment of Sex Offenders with Antiandrogen Medication: Conceptualization, Review of Treatment Modalities, and Preliminary Findings." **American Journal of Psychiatry,** 138(5): 601-607, May 1981.

The rationale for treating sexual offenders medically rather than punitively is reviewed. Special emphasis is focused on the use of antiandrogen drugs such as medroxyprogesterone acetate (Depo-Provera) which the literature shows has demonstrated success in reducing deviant sexual arousal and behavior.

383. Bradford, J.M.W. "Organic Treatments for the Male Sexual Offender." **Behavioral Sciences and the Law,** 3(4): 355-375, August 1985.

A variety of organic treatment for sexual offenders, including child molesters, is reviewed. These include administration of antiandrogen drugs, surgical castration, and stereotaxic neurosurgery.

384. Cordoba, O.A. and Chapel, J.L. "Medroxyprogesterone Acetate Antiandrogen Treatment of Hypersexuality in a Pedophiliac Sex Offender." **American Journal of Psychiatry,** 140(8): 1036-1039, August 1983.

A 25 year old chronic child molester was treated for five hundred days with medroxyprogesterone acetate (Depo-Provera) and reports a significant reduction in his sexual drive. Unpleasant side effects of the drug, including weight gain and fatigue, are also discussed.

385. Pinta, E.R. "Treatment of Obsessive Homosexual Pedophilic Fantasies with Medroxyprogesterone Acetate." **Biological Psychiatry,** 13(3): 369-373, June 1978.

A significant decrease in the intensity of homosexual pedophilic fantasies is noted for a 31 year old incarcerated child molester who was given repeated doeses of medroxyprogesterone acetate (Depo-Provera).

386. Spodak, M.K.; Falck, Z.A.; and Rappeport, J.R. "The Hormonal Treatment of Paraphiliacs with Depo-Provera." **Criminal Justice and Behavior,** 5(4): 304-314, December 1978.

The literature on the treatment of sexually deviant subjects with medroxyprogesterone acetate (Depo-Provera) is reviewed. Most of the studies show positive results that include decreases in erotic imagery, frequency of erections, and frequency of sexually deviant behavior. The drug's side effects include weight gain, fatigue, mood disturbances, and in some cases loss of body hair, and hot and cold flashes. In all cases, the side effects are reversible. Six patients, including four child molesters, are treated with Depo-Provera in this study and a favorable outcome is reported for three of the cases.

387. Tennent, G.; Bancroft, J.; and Cass, J. "The Control of Deviant Sexual Behavior by Drugs: A Double-Blind Controlled Study." **Archives of Sexual Behavior,** 3(3): 261-271, May 1974.

A double-blind study was conducted in which the effects of benperidol in reducing deviant sexual drive are compared with a placebo. The subjects are 12 hospitalized child molesters whose sexual drive was assessed through an interest and activity rating scale, a semantic differential scale, and through phallometric measures. Results show that the child molesters receiving the benperidol have a slight reduction in the frequency of their sexual thoughts when compared to the placebo group. It is concluded that benperidol is not sufficient to control severe forms of antisocial sexually deviant behavior, but may be of some value in cases where the simple reduction in the frequency of deviant sexual thoughts would be beneficial.

Castration

388. Heim, N. "Sexual Behavior of Castrated Sex Offenders." **Archives of Sexual Behavior,** 10(1): 11-19, February 1981.

Information from a questionnaire sent to 39 West German sex offenders who had volunteered for surgical castration and who had been released into the community after their surgery, shows that the sexual responsiveness of castrated males is more varied than expected. Six of the 19 child molesters in this sample still practice masturbation and/or coitus, compared to 8 of the 11 rapists. A number of physiological and biochemical reasons for this unexpected finding are posited, and it is theorized that the practice of releasing castrated sex offenders six months after their surgery, based on the assumption that hormonal loss is complete, is unwise.

Problems with Behavioral Treatment

Behavioral treatments such as covert sensitization, biofeedback and orgasmic reconditioning are certainly not without their problems. One of the greatest concerns that emerges in the literature is the possibility of response faking; for example, the subject may state that his fantasies about children have been reduced or have disappeared, when in fact they have not, or he may in other ways manipulate the treatment process. The following studies examine that problem and assess the degree to which response faking may mitigate the positive results typically documented for the behavioral treatment of child molesters, and also discuss methodological problems in the studies published on this subject.

389. Avery-Clark, C.A. and Laws, D.R. "Differential Erection Response Patterns of Sexual Child Abusers to Stimuli Describing Activities with Children." **Behavior Therapy,** 15(1): 71-83, January 1984.

To test the hypothesis that phallometric measurements are effective in distinguishing between nonaggressive and violent child molesters, 31 convicted child molesters are grouped as either more dangerous or less dangerous according to raters who reviewed their records, psychological data, and police and court reports. Each subject then listened to audiotaped descriptions of sexual activities with children which varied on both sexual and aggressive dimensions while penile responses to the tapes were measured. Using a formula in which the highest average maximum percent erection response generated by aggressive cues is divided by the average maximum percent erection response generated by the consensual sexual activity audiotape, a Dangerous Child Abuser Index (DCAI) is developed. With the DCAI it is shown that most dangerous child molesters have a score almost twice as high as the nonviolent offenders. Results of this study support the hypothesis, even though half of the subjects are able to exert some conscious control over their responses. It is not believed, however, that this faking response significantly altered the outcome of this study.

390. Kilman, P.R.; Sabalis, R.F.; Gearing, M.L.; Bukstel, L.H.; and Scovern, A.W. "The Treatment of Sexual Paraphilias: A Review of the Outcome Research." **Journal of Sex Research,** 18(3): 193-252, August 1982.
Data on the treatment of deviant sexual behavior and the methodologies used in the studies are reviewed. Despite methodological shortcomings, almost all of the studies demonstrate positive results.

391. Laws, D.R. and Holmen, M.L. "Sexual Response Faking by Pedophiles." **Criminal Justice and Behavior,** 5(4): 343-356, December 1978.
This study examines how response faking can be accomplished by child molesters in experimental and in treatment situations. The case of a 37 year old chronic child molester is used to illustrate how by creating fantasies, masturbating, and by mechanically manipulating the instruments, responses to sexually explicit material can be faked.

392. Quinsey, V.L. "Methodological Issues in Evaluating the Effectiveness of Aversion Therapies for Institutionalized Child Molesters." **Canadian Psychologist,** 14(4): 350-361, October 1973.
Aversion therapy is a popular technique for treating institutionalized child molesters, but it poses methodological problems because the subjects' responses to it are not always related to sexual arousal and because responses can be faked.

Psychotherapy

Psychotherapy has not typically been the treatment of choice for dealing with child molesters. Some studies, however, report positive results with the use of traditional psychotherapy, both on an individual and a group basis.

393. Cohen, M.L. and Kozol, H.L. "Evaluation for Parole at a Sex Offender Treatment Center." **Federal Probation,** 30(3): 50-55, September 1966.
The clinical picture of all sex offenders, including child molesters, is that their antisocial and asocial behavior arises from defects in their ego skills, in their ability to tolerate frustration, and in their capacity to form healthy interpersonal relationships. As a consequence, they tend to be selfish, cynical, unable to work in social groups or to engage in goal-directed behavior, and infantile in their value system. Psychotherapy, then, must focus on moving the sexual offender from a pattern of immaturity and self-cen-

teredness towards greater social sensitivity, control, and freer emotional responsiveness.

394. Daum, J.M. "Young Sex Offenders: The Other Victims of Sexual Abuse." **Juvenile and Family Court Journal,** 36(1): 17-22, Spring 1985.

The public's anger with sexual offenses involving young children often denies the adolescent molester the opportunity to receive the therapy he requires. Various approaches to therapy are discussed.

395. Foxe, A.N. "Psychoanalysis of a Sodomist." **American Journal of Orthopsychiatry,** 11(1): 133-142, January 1941.

The successful psychoanalysis of an incarcerated homosexual child molester is described. The 37 year old man was convicted of sodomy with two boys in what is described as an attempt to act out his own lost boyhood. He had been molested himself at the age of eight by an older male, and had a variety of homosexual experiences throughout his adolescence.

396. Groth, A.N.; Hobson, W.F.; Lucey, K.P.; and St. Pierre, J. "Juvenile Sexual Offenders: Guidelines for Treatment." **International Journal of Offender Therapy and Comparative Criminology,** 25: 265-275, 1981.

Techniques and strategies for the treatment of juvenile sexual offenders are presented.

397. Hartman, V. "Group Psychotherapy with Sexually Deviant Offenders (Pedophiles) -- The Peer Group as an Instrument of Mutual Control." **Journal of Sex Research,** 1(1): 45-57, March 1965.

This study examines a group psychotherapy approach with child molesters who were diverted into therapy by the court. All of the group members display varying degrees of ego disintegration due to a feeling of sadistic rage directed against the mother-figure coupled with a defensive need for her continuing attention. Their child molesting behavior was largely ego syntonic. Group therapy concentrated on strengthening the ego function through the use of ego support mechanisms, including the control and support of the peer group.

398. Hartman, V. "Notes on Group Psychotherapy with Pedophiles." **Canadian Psychiatric Association Journal,** 10(4): 283-288, July/August 1965.

Child molestation is theorized to have stemmed from severe ego regression while under stress, combined with an intense fear of ego disintegration caused by sadistic rage toward the mother-figure. An analytically oriented therapy group that emphasizes reality testing, responsibility, impulse control, and relationship development is found to be successful in treating incarcerated child molesters.

399. Karpman, B. "A Case of Pedophilia Cured by Psychoanalysis." **Psychoanalytic Review,** 37(3): 235-276, July 1950.

The successful psychoanalytic treatment of a 27 year old chronic child molester is described. Through his therapy and through an analysis of fifty-one of his dreams, it was discovered that the man's sexual deviation developed because of a sexual trauma he had experienced at the age of six and which he had repressed.

400. Lang, R.A.; Lloyd, C.A.; and Fiqia, N.A. "Goal Attainment Scaling with Hospitalized Sexual Offenders." **Journal of Nervous and Mental Disease,** 173(9): 527-537, September 1985.

A method of goal attainment scaling is developed for the therapy of 46 convicted sexual offenders, including 17 heterosexual and 15 homosexual child molesters. Each treatment goal is operationally defined, stated in positive terms, and achievable in six to eight months; goal attainment is measured on a 5-point scale. This study shows excellent results in changing the deviant sexual behavior of the subjects.

401. Langevin, R. and Lang, R.A. "Psychological Treatment of Pedophiles." **Behavioral Sciences and the Law,** 3(4): 403-419, August 1985.

A review of the literature shows that 78% of the published studies on the treatment of child molesters describe an aversive conditioning approach. This paper suggests that psychotherapy is a viable alternative to that and that such therapeutic techniques as group therapy and clinical imagery techniques can be very successful in treating child molesters.

402. Miller, H.L. and Haney, J.R. "Behavioral and Traditional Therapy Applied to Pedophiliac Exhibitionism: A Case Study." **Psychological Reports,** 39(3, Pt. 2): 1119-1124, December 1976.

The subject is a 36 year old male with a history of child molesting and exhibitionism for which he has spent over twenty years in prisons or in mental hospitals. He is treated successfully with a combination of insight therapy, social skills training, and aversive conditioning.

403. Moore, H.A.; Zusman, J.; and Root, G.C. "Noninstitutional Treatment for Sex Offenders in Florida." **American Journal of Psychiatry,** 142(8): 964-967, August 1985.

Surveys of 63 community mental health programs in Florida reveal that they are treating a total of 919 sexual offenders, 33% of whom are child molesters. Only 21% of these patients are self-referred; the rest are under court order for treatment. The average length of therapy for child molesters in these community programs is ten months. It is recommended that research on child molesters include subjects from this setting rather than relying solely on incarcerated or hospitalized offenders; research on the efficacy of community treatment of sexual offenders and on the qualifications and training of the staff who treat them is also encouraged.

404. Peters, J.J.; Pedigo, J.M.; Steg, J.; and McKenna, J.J. "Group Psychotherapy of the Sex Offender." **Federal Probation,** 32(3): 41-45, September 1968.

The successful adjustment to community life of a sample of 92 sexual offenders, including child molesters, who had received intensive group psychotherapy was compared to a matched sample of sexual offenders who had received no therapy. The recidivism rate of the first group is significantly lower than that of the control group. The process of group therapy and the difficulties in working with this type of patient are also discussed.

405. Resnick, H.L. and Peters, J.J. "Outpatient Group Therapy with Convicted Pedophiles." **International Journal of Group Psychotherapy,** 17(2): 151-158, 1967.

The shock of arrest, trial, and conviction lowers the child molester's defensive barrier of rationalization and denial and renders him particularly amenable to therapy. It is recommended that psychotherapy begin immediately after conviction and that a group therapy modality be utilized in which the development of trust, the creation of peer relationships within the group, self-esteem issues, and the modification of deviant sexual behavior are the primary goals.

406. Rowan, E.L. and Rowan, J.B. "Developing a Treatment Program for Peddophiles." **Corrective and Social Psychiatry,** 31(2): 62-64, 1985.

Using Finkelhor and Araji's four factor model of pedophilia (see reference number **136**), a twelve week treatment program for child molesters was developed. The program stresses sex education, the development of social skills, the resolution of cognitive distortions regarding sex roles and sexual objects, the decrease of deviant sexual arousal, and an increase in nondeviant sexual arousal.

Family Therapy

407. Bastani, J.B. and Kentsmith, D.R. "Psychotherapy with Wives of Sexual Deviants." **American Journal of Psychotherapy,** 34(1): 20-25, January 1980.

Nine women who are married to sexually deviant males all express a fear of social condemnation because of their husbands' behavior. Believing that they had not sexually fulfilled their husbands, they blame themselves for the deviance. All of the women have a poor self-concept and a strong need for reassurance and approval. Poor relationships with their own mothers are noted and in all cases, their fathers are described as emotionally detached or physically absent. All of the women married early and although only two of the nine were aware of their husbands' behavior, most of the rest suspected but did or said nothing. The ego defenses of denial, rationalization, intellectualization, isolation of effect, and undoing are commonly noted. All of them clearly identified with their husbands' aggression and the roots of this repressed hostility towards women is found in their childhoods. Little empathy for their husbands' victims is noted. Five of the women are married to child molesters, and detailed case histories are given for two of them.

408. Hitchens, E.W. "Denial: An Identified Theme in the Marital Relationships of Sex Offenders." **Perspectives in Psychiatric Care,** 10(4): 152-159, October/November 1972.

Wives of hospitalized sex offenders were asked to join their husbands in therapy. Denial emerges as a major theme in their marriage relationship; as a defense, it protects the wives from the perception of and the confrontation with the unpleasant reality of their husbands' behavior. In addition, most of the women question their own sexual attractiveness and self-worth. Psychodrama and confrontation are used in therapy to address and resolve these issues.

Other Therapy Approaches

409. Corsini, R.J. "Psychodramatic Treatment of a Pedophile." **Group Psychotherapy,** 4(3): 166-171, December 1951.

An incarcerated child molester is able to understand the motives behind his sexual behavior and more openly discuss his feelings and fears by participating in a psychodrama group in prison.

410. Stava, L. "The Use of Hypnotic Uncovering Techniques in the Treatment of Pedophilia." **International Journal of Clinical and Experimental Hypnosis,** 32(4): 350-355, October 1984.

The use of hypnotic uncovering techniques is demonstrated to be a successful method to reduce sexual attraction to children in a group of five child molesters.

Treatment Programs

411. Serber, M. and Keith, C.G. "The Atascadero Project: Model of a Sexual Re-Training Program for Incarcerated Homosexual Pedophiles." **Journal of Homosexuality,** 1(1): 87-97, Fall 1974.

A behavioral retraining group for incarcerated homosexual child molesters teaches social interaction skills through consciousness-raising, role-playing, and assertiveness training techniques.

412. Wolfe, R.W. and Marino, D.R. "A Program of Behavior Treatment for Incarcerated Pedophiles." **American Criminal Law Review,** 13(1): 69-84, Summer 1975.

The program of the Mental Hygiene Unit of the Connecticut Correctional Institution for the treatment of child molesters is described. The program is built on the philosophy that pedophilic behavior is learned and that it therefore can be unlearned through a combination of aversive conditioning, covert sensitization, and group therapy. Successful results are documented for the 28 subjects in this study.

A wide variety of therapeutic modalities for treating molested children is presented in the literature. Each technique is generally predicated upon the assumptions that the children's immediate reaction to the molestation, depending of course on its nature and chronicity, is likely to be traumatic in nature; and on the possibility that the molestation may produce a sequela of psychological and behavioral effects that will have an adverse impact on adolescent and adult adjustment.

The following references examine the immediate and longterm therapeutic strategies for intervening in cases of child molestation.

General Treatment Considerations

413. Conte, J.R. "Progress in Treating the Sexual Abuse of Children." **Social Work**, 29(3): 258-262, May/June 1984.
　　Data from published studies are presented to challenge the belief that child molesters constitute a different clinical category from incestuous males. Another prevalent belief, that child molestation should be only a mental health problem, is questioned as well; the economic, cultural, religious and social factors that support this behavior and prevent intervention must be recognized. Finally, stages of professional intervention and drawbacks in each stage are discussed.

414. Funk, J.B. "Management of Sexual Molestation in Preschoolers." **Clinical Pediatrics**, 19(10): 686-688, October 1980.
　　A single incident of nonviolent sexual molestation usually is not psychologically harmful to children. In cases like that, parents should be reassured of that fact and should be allowed to express their feelings and fears. It is helpful for the therapist to give parents factual information and hints as to how to communicate with their child about this incident. If necessary, a referral should be made to a treatment agency.

415. Funk, J.B. "Consultation in the Management of Sexual Molestation." **Journal of Clinical Child Psychology,** 10(1): 83-85, Summer 1981.

Consultive procedures in cases of child molestation are presented. In order for mental health practitioners to be helpful to molested children and their families, the consultant should help them explore their own feelings and comfort level in managing this kind of problem, and give them information about child molestation, and assist them in developing treatment plans. Because the reactions of parents or caregivers to the molestation are significant to the child's reactions, focus is placed on helping mental health professionals work with parents.

416. Furniss, T. "Mutual Influence and Interlocking Professional-Family Process in the Treatment of Child Sexual Abuse and Incest." **Child Abuse and Neglect,** 7(2): 207-223, 1983.

Three types of intervention -- police, social service, and therapeutic -- are described and the effects that each has on the family and the child in cases of sexual molestation are discussed. A model for the interlocking of the system in order to serve families and children is proposed.

417. James, O.W. "The Management of a Sexually Charged Clinical Problem: Social Structural and Psychoanalytic Functionalist Approaches in a Therapeutic Community." **British Journal of Medical Psychology,** 59(1): 27-34, March 1986.

A five year old girl's disclosure of an incident of sexual molestation by a fifteen year old male is analyzed within the frameworks of both structuralist theory and psychoanalytic functionalism. Both the child and the adolescent perpetrators are residents of a therapeutic community.

418. Kiefer, C.R. "Sexual Molestation of a Child." **Medical Aspects of Human Sexuality,** 7(12): 127-128, December 1973.

The child often plays some part in encouraging the sexual molestation; their normal curiosity includes a fascination with their bodies and with sexual behavior. Treatment, therefore, must be sensitive to the child's role in the molestation and the resulting guilt feelings. The child's parents need to be therapeutically dealt with as well.

419. Lamb, S. "Treating Sexually Abused Children: Issues of Blame and Responsibility." **American Journal of Orthopsychiatry,** 56(2): 303-307, April 1986.

The thesis of this study is that the traditional therapeutic practice of reassuring sexually molested children that the molestation was not their fault actually reinforces their feelings of powerlessness and lack of control. Therapists are advised to work with children in showing them the chain of choices and events that have led up to the sexual contact, and to assist them in exercising good decision making and healthy options in the event they are faced with such incidents again. Such an approach is critical to the development of feelings of power and control which are likely to have been subverted by the molestation.

420. Litin, E.M.; Giffin, M.; and Johnson, A. "Parental Influence in Unusual Sexual Behavior in Children." **Psychoanalytic Quarterly**, 25: 37-55, 1956.

The role of the therapist in the evaluation and treatment of sexually molested children is discussed. Therapists are warned that an insistence that a patient's memory of molestation is really a fantasy may drive the patient out of therapy and even into psychosis.

421. MacFarlane, K. and Bulkley, J. "Treating Child Sexual Abuse: An Overview of Current Treatment Program Models." **Journal of Social Work and Human Sexuality**, 1(1-2): 69-91, Fall/Winter 1982.

In 1981 there were over five hundred treatment centers across the country that specialize in child sexual abuse. Program models, philosophies, and treatment strategies of the various types of agencies are described.

422. Paulson, M. "Incest and Sexual Molestation: Clinical and Legal Issues." **Journal of Clinical Child Psychology**, 7(3): 177-180, Fall 1978.

The UCLA Child Trauma Intervention Project, a multicultural, bilingual program for the diagnosis and treatment of incestuous and nonincestuous child molestation is described.

423. Rosenfeld, A.A.; Krieger, M.J.; Nadelson, C.; and Blackman, J. "The Sexual Misuse of Children." **Psychiatric Opinion**, 13(2): 6-12, April 1976.

Strategies for the evaluation and treatment of sexually misused children are discussed.

424. Stokes, R.E. "A Research Approach to Sexual Offenses Involving Children." **Canadian Journal of Corrections**, 6(1): 87-94, January 1964.

Most of the children who were molested by the 55 child molesters in this sample were attractive and had pleasing personalities. Some of them, in fact, appeared intolerant of denial of satisfaction and seemed to possess unusually strong desires. Given this profile, the children do not entirely deserve to be called innocent victims, and some of them clearly initiated the sexual contact.

Psychotherapy With Children

425. MacVicar, K. "Psychotherapeutic Issues in the Treatment of Sexually Abused Girls." **Journal of the American Academy of Child Psychiatry**, 18(2): 342-353, Spring 1979.

Based upon a sample of 17 sexually molested latency age girls, it is obvious that the girls can be divided into two type of victims: accidental and participant. The former were molested only once and by a stranger or a near stranger; they promptly reported the molestation and had their families' support throughout the disclosure and the therapy that followed. They tended to have symptoms of secondary phobias, disturbing dreams, and depressive symptoms which were quite amendable to brief psychotherapy. The participant victims, on the other hand, were molested multiple times over periods of weeks to years, were coerced into keeping the molestation secret by the perpetrator who frequently was a family member, and tended to show symptoms of guilt, hostility, sexual acting out, and depression.

426. Schoettle, U.C. "Child Exploitation: A Study of Child Pornography." **American Academy of Child Psychiatry**, 19(2): 289-299, Spring 1980.
The case of a 12 year old girl whose sexual acts with other children and with adults were photographed and filmed is presented. The child was of low average intelligence, and described feelings of helplessness, anxiety, and depression, and came from a chaotically disorganized family. Therapy proceeded in three stages: dealing with feelings of guilt, anxiety and loss of self-esteem; resolving the problems in the parent-child relationship; and resuming the normal developmental process.

427. Schoettle, U.C. "Treatment of the Child Pornography Patient." **American Journal of Psychiatry,** 137(9): 1109-1110, September 1980.
Therapy with a 12 year old girl who had been involved in a child pornography ring in which she was photographed in sexual acts with other children and with adults is described. Therapy proceeded in three stages: dealing with overwhelming and often immobilizing feelings; addressing problems in the parent-child relationship; and finally integrating the child back into a normal lifestyle.

428. Slager-Jorne, P. "Counseling Sexually Abused Children." **Personnel and Guidance Journal**, 57(2): 103-105, October 1978.
Five cases of sexually molested children are presented. Each experienced anxiety which created phobias, tics, nightmares, enuresis, eating disorders and sexual acting out. Therapists are encouraged to create a supportive, understanding environment in which presenting symptoms are treated and the child is able and willing to discuss the sexual molestation.

429. Sturkie, K. "Structured Group Treatment for Sexually Abused Children." **Health and Social Work**, 8(4): 299-308, Fall 1983.
A therapy group for latency age sexually molested children is described. The group lasts eight weeks and deals with eight significant issues in the lives of molested children: believability; guilt and responsibility; body integrity and protection; secrecy and sharing; anger; powerlessness; other life crises, tasks and symptoms; and court attendance and testimony.

Special Therapeutic Techniques

430. Burgess, A.W.; McCausland, M.P.; and Wolbert, W.A. "Children's Drawings as Indicators of Sexual Trauma." **Perspectives in Psychiatric Care,** 19(2): 50-58, March/April 1981.
Drawings of sexually molested children are used to assess the degree of trauma the child has experienced and to gauge the child's progress in resolving molestation-related issues during therapy.

431. Hall, N.M. "Group Treatment for Sexually Abused Children." **Nursing Clinics of North America.** 13(4): 701-705, December 1978.

A six week long, issue oriented group counseling program for young sexually molested children is described.

432. Kelley, S.J. "The Use of Art Therapy with Sexually Abused Children." **Journal of Psychosocial Nursing,** 22(12): 12-18, December 1984.

Art therapy is a useful and nonthreatening modality for the expression of the feelings of the sexually molested child. The drawings of ten sexually molested children as they progress through therapy are presented and analyzed.

433. Weeks, R.B. "Counseling Parents of Sexually Abused Children." **Medical Aspects of Human Sexuality,** 10(8): 43-44, August 1976.

The first goal of treating sexually molested children is to protect them from further trauma; focusing on the parents of the children, then, becomes an important secondary goal. Parents should be advised to talk calmly and nonjudgmentally with their children about the alleged molestation, and after gathering some details, should then contact the police. Nightmares, regressive behavior, crying spells, eating disorders and unusual fears may be shown by the children.

CHAPTER 9:
LEGAL ISSUES

In recent years, the legal system has had to address the social problem of child molestation. Mandatory reporting laws, the revision of hearsay statutes, and innovations for using molested children as witnesses in a court of law are some of the approaches the system has had to develop in recent years. Attention has been paid as well to developing strategies for the coordination of the various systems that will intervene in cases of child molestation.

Laws

434. Besharov, D.J. "Unfounded Allegations -- A New Child Abuse Problem." **Public Interest,** 83: 18-33, Spring 1986.
The last decade has seen a great success in raising the public's consciousness about child abuse and has witnessed a significant increase in the number of cases of child abuse reported to authorities. Mandatory reporting laws and the vague definition of child abuse, however, have created a flood of unfounded allegations that have overwhelmed the resources of protective service and law enforcement agencies. This problem is further confounded by the media's often hysterical reporting of sensational cases, by child abuse prevention programs, and by the availability of child abuse hotline numbers, as well as by a wealth of published information that generates a whole list of vaguely worded symptoms or indicators of child abuse. In order to focus limited resources on true cases of child abuse, it is recommended that reporting laws and associated educational materials and prevention programs be improved so that they provide practical and realistic guidance as to what cases should be reported; that the liability provisions of state reporting laws be modified; that child abuse hotlines concentrate on fulfilling their responsibility to screen reports so unfounded reports will not be investigated; and that the federal government update its policies and funding priorities.

435. Bradmiller, L.L. and Walters, W.S. "Seriousness of Sexual Assault Charges." **Criminal Justice and Behavior,** 12(4): 463-484, December 1985.

A Forensic Case Rating Scale was developed to quantify materials found in the records of 89 sex offenders convicted in Hamilton County, Ohio, and to determine which of these variables are related to the seriousness of the criminal charge. Although the apparent goal of the law against the sexual molestation of children is to allow prosecution to the fullest possible extent, the study shows that the age of the victim is not a variable in predicting the seriousness of the charge. The use of force and the type of sexual activity emerge as powerful predictors of the seriousness of the charge.

436. Conte, J.R. and Berliner, L. "Prosecution of the Offender in Cases of Sexual Assault Against Children." **Victimology: An International Journal,** 6(1-4): 102-109, 1981.
Eighty-four cases of child molestation prosecuted in Seattle, Washington in 1978 are analyzed; slightly over half of these cases involved molestation by a nonfamily person. Case analysis shows that most child molesters plead guilty to the original charge if the sentence does not mandate a prison sentence; their guilty plea keeps the child out of court. Probation is the most likely disposition, and counseling while on probation is required for most of the cases.

437. MacNamara, D.E.J. "Sex Offenses and Sex Offenders." **Annals of the American Academy of Political and Social Science,** 376(1): 148-155, March 1968.
Although laws against certain types of sexual behavior are rooted in a patriarchal sociosexual culture, and do not accurately depict either the incidence or the modes of sexual conduct, laws against adult sexual behavior with children should not be repealed, especially in the absence of effective therapeutic techniques with offenders.

438. Mangus, A.R. "Sexual Deviation Research in California." **Sociology and Social Research,** 37(3): 175-181, January/February 1953.
After two sexually motivated murders of young children in Los Angeles, California in 1949, the Governor called a special session of the state legislature to consider the development of laws against a variety of sexual offenses. After public hearings and written testimony, the subcommittee found that most sexual practices were already proscribed by law and that what was needed was more knowledge about the nature and extent of sexual offenses, not more legislation against them. To that end, the legislature allocated money for research into sexual crimes.

439. Massey, D.C. "No First Amendment Protection for the Sexploitation of Children." **Loyola Law Review,** 29(1): 227-235, Winter 1983.
This paper reviews various state court decisions regarding child pornography.

440. Shouvlin, D.P. "Preventing the Sexual Exploitation of Children: A Model Act." **Wake Forest Law Review,** 17(4): 536-560, August 1981.
Model laws from the state of North Carolina that clearly define child

sexual exploitation and cover the entire range of sexual acts that may be involved are described.

441. Slovenko, R. "Statutory Rape." **Medical Aspects of Human Sexuality,** 5(3): 154, 166, March 1971.

Since statutory rape laws do not consider the issues of consent and the child's prior sexual behavior, they should be considered obsolete concepts. Some recent changes in the laws throughout the country are reviewed.

442. Stack, E.J. "Preventing the Sexual Exploitation of Children: The New York Experience." **New York State Bar Journal,** 56(2): 11-18, February 1984.

In 1982, the United States Supreme Court upheld the constitutionality of the *New York v. Ferber* case which proscribed the promotion and distribution of material depicting children under sixteen in sexual activities, whether the material was legally obscene or not. The development of this legislation and the impact it has had since the Supreme Court decision are outlined.

443. Williams, J.E.H. "Sex Offenses: The British Experience." **Law and Contemporary Problems** 25(2): 334-360, Spring 1960.

The British experience with the government subsidized study of deviant sexual behavior and the law's response to it are reviewed, with special attention to those committees that examined sexual offenses against young people, prostitution, and homosexuality. The Committee on Sexual Offenses Against Young Persons convened in 1925 to collect information about the prevalence of child molestation and the legal penalties for such behavior. The Committee made forty-three recommendations, few of which were ever implemented. Among those recommendations were that trial procedures should be designed in such a way as to protect victimized children who must testify; that the age of consent for females should be raised from sixteen to seventeen, and that mandatory psychiatric examinations be conducted on all sexual offenders.

System Intervention

444. Adams-Tucker, C. "The Unmet Psychiatric Needs of Sexually Abused Youths: Referrals from a Child Protection Agency and Clinical Evaluations." **Journal of the American Academy of Child Psychiatry,** 23(6): 659-667, November 1984.

A comparison of a group of 25 sexually molested children who had received psychiatric evaluations with a group of 201 children whose alleged sexual molestation was referred to a Child Protection Agency reveals that the decision to refer a child for evaluation is based on a number of unexpected variables. Children who had their first molestation experience under the age of ten were more likely to be referred for evaluation than older children; white girls were referred the most often, regardless of age, and no black boy was referred for evaluation. Although there are no significant differences in socioeconomic level between the two groups, data analysis shows that children from two-parent families are much more often referred for evaluation than children from single parent families. Of the 25 children referred for psychiatric evaluation, 24 were diagnosed according to DSM-III nomenclature, with adjustment disorders and behavioral disorders most commonly diagnosed. It was also discovered that screening devices and judgment calls on the parts of the professionals in the Child Protection Agency dismissed 43% of the cases of alleged sexual abuse reported to them as unfounded.

445. Arthur, L.G. "Child Sexual Abuse: Improving the System's Response." **Juvenile and Family Court Journal,** 37(2): 1-75, 1986.

The entire issue of this journal is devoted to an examination of both child molestation and incest, with sections on the nature of the problem, detection, intervention, interviewing children and family members, protecting the children, court procedures, and sentences and dispositions of child molesters.

446. Conte, J.R. "The Justice System and Sexual Abuse of Children." **Social Service Review,** 58(4): 556-568, December 1984.

Professionals who work with sexually molested children must examine some of their preconceived notions about sexual abuse and help develop a justice system response that operates on facts and on advocacy for children.

447. DeJong, A.R. "The Medical Evaluation of Sexual Abuse in Children." **Hospital and Community Psychiatry,** 36(5): 509-512, May 1985.

The lack of physicians' training in identifying the symptoms of sexual molestation in children, the stress that is produced by their discovery and identification of molested children, and the frustrations produced by unsatisfying interactions with the social service delivery network are factors that contribute to physicians' failure to recognize sexual molestation and/or to report it.

448. Fontana, V.J. "When Systems Fail: Protecting the Victim of Child Sexual Abuse." **Children Today,** 13(4): 14-18, July/August 1984.

Problems with the definition of child sexual abuse, the laws and conditions regarding its reporting, the stigma of disclosure, and the conflicts in philosophy as to how the perpetrator should be treated or punished are all barriers to prompt and effective system intervention.

449. Labai, D. "The Protection of the Child Victim of a Sexual Offense in the Criminal Justice System." **Wayne Law Review,** 15: 927-1032, 1969.

The degree of psychic trauma to the child who has been sexually molested is dependent to some extent on the way he or she is treated after the disclosure or the discovery of the molestation. "Legal system trauma" can be generated by the insensitive handling of these cases. The appointment and training of special police officers to deal with these children can serve three cardinal purposes: the protection of the children's welfare; the guarantee of better methods of recording the children's statements; and the contribution to the quality and trustworthiness of police reports in court. All elements of the criminal justice system must be responsive to the needs of molested children. Several innovative programs based on the procedures used in Israel and Denmark in cases of child molestation are decribed in detail.

450. Schultz, LG. "The Child Sex Victim: Social, Psychological, and Legal Perspectives." **Child Welfare,** 52(3): 147-157, March 1973.

Generally, sexual assaults on children do not have excessively unsettling effects on the children's personality development nor on their adult adjustment. The most damaging effects are created by the disclosure of the sexual molestation and the resultant legal and social service sytem interventions.

451. Stone, L.E.; Tyler, R.P.; and Mead J.J. "Law Enforcement Officers as Investigators and Therapists in Child Sexual Abuse: A Training Model." **Child Abuse and Neglect,** 8(1): 75-82, 1984.

A six hour training module on child sexual abuse for law enforcement officers is described. Sessions cover the dynamics of child sexual abuse, the physical examination and the collection of evidence, and interviewing techniques.

452. Wenck, E.O. "Sexual Child Abuse: An American Shame That Can Be Changed." **Capital University Law Review,** 12(3): 355-367, Fall 1983.

The work of the Sex Offenses Task Force of Baltimore, Mayland to improve the criminal justice system's intervention in cases of child molestation is described.

Children's Testimony in Court

One of the most pressing concerns in the legal system has to do with the molested child's testimony in court. Under the pressure of cross-examination, and in the presence of strangers who may be skeptical of the allegation, the molested child can experience considerable problems and stresses when he or she is required to testify.

The following references examine this "legal system trauma" and suggest ways in which it can be reduced. Innovations such as having the child testify via a closed circuit television or on videotape hold promise for reducing that trauma, but also raise Constitutional issues in light of the defendant's Sixth Amendment right to confront accusing witnesses.

453. Avery, M. "The Child Abuse Witness: Potential for Secondary Victimization." **Criminal Justice Journal,** 7(1): 1-48, Fall 1983.

The difficulties in using sexually molested children as witnesses in a court of law are discussed. Such innovations as having the children testify on two-way closed circuit television or on videotape are presented.

454. Bainor, M.H. "The Constitutionality of the Use of Two-Way Closed Circuit Television to Take Testimony of Child Victims of Sex Crimes." **Fordham Law Review,** 53(5): 995-1018, April 1985.

It is argued that allowing the molested child to testify via a two-way closed circuit television in a separate room from the defendant is the best way to prosecute a case without diminishing the defendant's 6th Amendment rights to confront witnesses against him or her.

455. Bauer, H. "Preparation of the Sexually Abused Child for Court Testimony." **Bulletin of the American Academy of Psychiatry and the Law,** 11(3): 287-289, 1983.

Techniques and strategies for reducing the anxiety of young sexually molested children as they testify in a court of law are described.

456. Berliner, L. and Barbieri, M.K. "The Testimony of the Child Victim of Sexual Assault." **Journal of Social Issues,** 40(2): 125-137, Spring 1984.

Although children's reliability and credibility as witnesses in a court of law are routinely questioned, there is no evidence to support that skepticism, and none to prove that children often make false allegations of sexual molestation. Preparing children for court testimony and the legal problems with such testimony are discussed.

457. Bulkley, J.A. "Evidentiary and Procedural Trends in State Legislation and Other Emerging Legal Issues in Child Sexual Abuse Cases." **Dickinson Law Review,** 89(3): 645-668, Spring 1985.

The statutory reforms to improve the handling of child sexual abuse cases in various states are reviewed.

458. Eatman, R. "Minor Victims of Sexual Assault." **New Hampshire Bar Journal,** 26(3): 199-214, Spring 1985.

The difficulties in using sexually molested children as witnesses in a court of law are presented and strategies for reducing their anxiety about testifying are suggested.

459. Eatman, R. "Videotaping Interviews with Child Sex Offense Victims." **Children's Legal Rights Journal,** 7(1): 13-17, Winter 1986.

Videotaping interviews with children who have been sexually molested can be a useful adjunct to investigation, court testimony, and to therapy, but jurisdictions must carefully establish a protocol before this process is widely used. It is advised that the state's discovery privilege, confidentiality, and evidentiary rules be researched as a first step, and that special attention be paid to the legal requirements of the state's hearsay rule and the 6th Amendment confrontation clause. Then a procedure can be developed for identifying those cases in which videotaped interviews would be beneficial.

460. (Editorial Note). "The Testimony of Child Victims in Sex Abuse Prosecution: Two Legislative Innovations." **Harvard Law Review,** 98(4): 806-827, February 1985.

State legislatures have recognized the problems with prosecuting cases of child molestation and generally have acted to strengthen the prosecutors' hand while at the same time easing the burden the judicial system places on the child witness. Two major innovations in this area - the development of hearsay statutes and videotaping statutes - are discussed in detail. The legal problems each poses, most notably the possible violation of the defendants' 6th Amendment right of confrontation, are outlined and discussed.

461. Henriques, B. and Wells, N.H. "Sexual Assaults on Children." **British Medical Journal,** 2(5267): 1628-1633, December 16, 1961.

To reduce the difficulties a molested child has in testifying in court, it is advised that the courtroom be cleared of press and spectators, and that the child be allowed to take a modified form of the oath. It is also suggested that child molestation cases have priority for prosecution so that delays do not increase the anxiety a child is likely to experience.

462. Jones, D.P.H. and Krugman, R.D. "Can A Three Year Old Child Bear Witness to Her Sexual Assault and Attempted Murder?" **Child Abuse and Neglect,** 10(2): 253-258, 1986.

A three year old child who was abducted from in front of her home, sexually molested, and then abandoned in a sewage pit at the bottom of a mountain outhouse, was an excellent and reliable witness as to the details of her experience and the identity of her abductor. That reliability was consistent throughout the months of investigation, and up until the time the trial was scheduled, nearly a year and a half later. The perpetrator confessed just before the trial and was sentenced to ten years in prison.

463. Kelly, J.L. "Legislative Responses to Child Sexual Abuse Cases: The Hearsay Exception and the Videotape Deposition." **Catholic University Law Review.** 34(4): 1021-1054, Summer 1985.

This paper examines such statutory alternatives to in-court testimony of child victims of sexual molestation as videotaped testimony, and testimony via a two-way closed circuit television. The defendant's 6th Amendment rights to confront his or her accuser are analyzed in relation to these alternatives.

464. Mahady-Smith, C.M. "The Young Victim as Witness for the Prosecution: Another Form of Abuse." **Dickinson Law Review,** 89(3): 721-749, Spring 1985.

The difficulties encountered during trial when a sexually molested child must testify as a witness are discussed. The scope and history of Pennsylvania's Greenleaf Bill which allows for videotaped tesimony, the designation of qualified child advocates to act on behalf of the child who is involved with the criminal justice system, and that creates greater latitude in the admission of a child's out-of-court statements about the molestation are presented.

465. McGrath, M. and Clemens, C. "The Child Victim as Witness in Sexual Abuse Cases." **Montana Law Review,** 46(2): 229-243, Summer 1985.

Evidentiary problems that commonly occur in cases of child molestation are discussed, and such alternatives to traditionally prosecuted cases as videotaped testimony and testimony on two-way closed circuit television are presented.

466. Melton, G.B. "Sexually Abused Children and the Legal System: Some Policy Recommendations." **American Journal of Family Therapy,** 13(1): 61-66, 1985.

The competency of children to testify in court is discussed, and evidentiary rules to protect children are suggested.

467. Mertens, R. "Child Sexual Abuse in California: Legislative and Judicial Responses." **Golden Gate University Law Review,** 15(3): 437-491, Fall 1985.

The recent and proposed changes in California law regarding hearsay exceptions, expert testimony, and videotaped testimony in cases of child molestation are discussed.

468. (Note). "Minnesota's Hearsay Exception for Child Victims of Sexual Abuse." **William Mitchell Law Review,** 11(3): 799-823, 1985.

This paper reviews Minnesota Statutes section 595.02, subdivision 3, which allows for the admission of some out-of-court statements made by children who had been molested. The statute also provides for the videotaped testimony of the children under adversarial conditions that protect the 6th Amendment right of the defendant to confront a witness.

469. Oseid, J. "Defendants' Rights in Child Witness Competency Hearings: Establishing Constitutional Procedures for Sexual Abuse Cases." **Minnesota Law Review,** 69(6): 1377-1399, June 1985.

In most states, a child victim's competency to testify in a criminal trial must be determined in what is often an informal pretrial hearing by a judge. This paper examines the defendant's Constitutional rights in this competency hearing and urges that states develop a formal procedure so that the rights both of the child and the defendant can be protected.

470. Reifen, D. "Protection of Children Involved in Sexual Offenses: A New Method of Investigation in Israel." **Journal of Criminal Law, Criminology, and Police Science,** 49(3): 222-229, September/October 1958.

The role of the Israeli Youth Examiner, a specially trained mental health expert, in the investigation and the trial in cases of child molestation, is outlined.

471. Schultz, L.G. "Psychotherapeutic and Legal Approaches to the Sexually Victimized Child." **International Journal of Child Psychotherapy,** 1(4): 115-128, October 1972.

Since the cross-examination of a sexually abused child in a court of law can be an experience that is more traumatizing than the molestation itself, it is advised that therapists be used as adjuncts and as expert witnesses during the trial.

472. Skoler, G. "New Hearsay Exceptions for a Child's Statement of Sexual Abuse." **John Marshall Law Review,** 18: 1-48, 1984.

The videotaped testimony in a court of law of sexually molested children is discussed. Constitutional arguments for and against such a procedure are made, and the ramifications of such a practice in daily trial procedures are discussed.

473. Waterman, C.K. and Foss-Goodman, D. "Child Molestation: Variables Relating to Attribution of Fault to Victims, Offenders, and Nonparticipating Parents." **Journal of Sex Research,** 20(4): 329-349, November 1984.

A group of 180 male and 180 female college students read descriptions of an act of child molestation in which the child's age and relationship to the adult perpetrator were varied, and then indicated how much fault they attributed to each person in the scenario and why they assessed that amount of fault. Students also took a survey which indicated their tendency for sex-role stereotyping, their adversarial sexual beliefs, their sexual conservatism, and their acceptance of interpersonal violence. Analysis of the data shows that males attribute more fault to the children, and that sexual conservatism and acceptance of interpersonal violence are factors that predict victim blame. Students who had been molested as children tended to blame the child victim less than did those students who had not been molested.

474. Weiss, E.H. and Berg, R.F. "Child Victims of Sexual Assault: Impact of Court Procedures." **Journal of the American Academy of Child Psychiatry,** 21(5): 513-518, September 1982.

Strategies for assessing the child's emotional reaction to the sexual molestation and for preparing the child for court testimony are discussed. It is recommended that the mental health system play an advocacy role on behalf of the sexually molested child and that it work towards changes in the legal system that will reduce the trauma a child so often experiences when made to testify in court.

475. Wise, D.R. "Child Witness: The Constitutionality of Admitting the Videotape Testimony at Trial of Sexually Abused Children." **Whittier Law Review,** 7(2): 639-661, 1985.

The defendant's 6th Amendment rights to confront a witness against him or her in a court of law are analyzed within the framework of recent legislation in various states that allow the child's testimony to be videotaped so the child does not have to appear in court.

476. Yun, J. "A Comprehensive Approach to Child Hearsay Statements in Sex Abuse Cases." **Columbia Law Review,** 83(7): 1745-1766, November 1983.

The traditional basis of the hearsay rule and the underlying logic to its exception are examined within the framework of sexually molested children who must testify as witnesses in a court of law. An alternative model, based on the one that has been implemented in the state of Washington, is proposed; in this model, children's out-of-court statements about the molestation are admitted into evidence if their time, content, and circumstances provide sufficient indicia of reliability.

Mandatory Reporting

477. James, J.; Womack, W.M.; and Strauss, F. "Physician Reporting of Sexual Abuse of Children." **Journal of the American Medical Association,** 240(11): 1145-1146, September 1978.

A random sample of 600 pediatricians and general practitioners in Seattle, Washington was sent a questionnaire eliciting information regarding their frequency of contact with sexually molested children, the types of sexual abuse encountered in their practice, their procedure for reporting, and the treatment or referral for treatment provided. Replies tabulated for the 96 returned surveys indicate that over half of the respondents saw at least one sexually molested child a year in their practice, and treated from one to seven suspected cases each year. Over one-half of these children are judged by the physicians to have been seriously to very seriously traumatized by the molestation, yet only 42% of the physicians reply that they would report any case of child sexual abuse, despite a mandatory reporting law in that state. The reluctance to report reflects the respondents' dissatisfaction with social service agency intervention in these cases, and their opinion that such intervention actually would be more harmful than beneficial to the child and his or her family.

478. Saulsbury, F.T. "Evaluation of Child Abuse by Reporting Physicians." **American Journal of Diseases of Children,** 139(4): 393-395, 1985.

A sample of 511 physicians was surveyed in Virginia; 311 returned a questionnaire that asked about their reporting of sexual, physical, and emotional abuse of child patients. Over half of the responding physicians stated that they had seen no cases of child abuse in the past year. Most of the physicians stated that they are more inclined to report sexual abuse than any other kind of abuse, and few stated any reluctance in working with outside social service agencies. No relationship between reporting tendencies, the age of the physician, his or her specialty, number of years in practice, or characteristics of the practice or population in the surrounding area was found.

Other Considerations

479. Beaty, P.T. and Woolley, M.R. "Child Molesters Need Not Apply: A History of Pennsylvania's Child Protective Services Law and Legislative Efforts to Prevent the Hiring of Abusers by Child Care Agencies." **Dickinson Law Review**, 89(3): 669-719, Spring 1985.

The history of the legislation that culminated in the Child Protective Services Law of 1975 in the state of Pennsylvania is reviewed. The 1984 amendment to that law, Act 224, which requires operators of child care facilities to check with a statewide central register of convicted child molesters before hiring an employee, is also described.

480. Benedek, E.P. "The Role of the Child Psychiatrist in Court Cases Involving Child Victims of Sexual Assault." **Journal of the American Academy of Child Psychiatry**, 21(5): 519-520, September 1982.

The role of the child psychiatrist in cases of child molestation should be mutidimensional in nature. It is recommended that psychiatrists take an active role not only in evaluating and treating molested children and their families, but also in serving as an expert witness in a court of law, in preparing the children for court testimony, and in educating the judge, law enforcement officers, and attorneys in the dynamics and effects of child molestation.

481. Davidson, H. "Protection of Children through Criminal History Record-Screening: Well-Meaning Promises and Legal Pitfalls." **Dickinson Law Review**, 89(3): 577-603, Spring 1985.

This paper examines the legislative history of mandating criminal record checks of potential employees in day care and in other juvenile facilities in order to protect children from sexual abuse by people who are caregivers. It concludes that this safety check is a necessary precaution, but that its helpfulness in identifying people who might molest children is greatly overrated. The legal issues raised by these checks are also analyzed.

482. Leake, H.C. and Smith, D.J. "Preparing for and Testifying in a Child Abuse Hearing." **Clinical Pediatrics**, 16(11): 1057-1063, November 1977.

The physician's role in child abuse court hearings is described. The preparation of notes, the demeanor on the stand, and the most common legal strategies for discrediting the physician's testimony are discussed.

483. Finkelhor, D. "What's Wrong with Sex Between Adults and Children?" **American Journal of Orthopsychiatry**, 49(4): 692-697, October 1979.

Intuitive arguments against sex between adults and children include the argument that it is intrinsically wrong from a biological and/or psychological point of view; that it entails the premature sexualization of children; and that it is damaging to children. Each of those arguments has some validity, but each, for various reasons, is also weak. A stronger and sounder line of reasoning for prohibiting such sexual contacts is that the fundamental conditions of consent cannot prevail because children lack the two components essential to voluntary consent: knowledge enough to make them completely informed, and the freedom to say yes or no to the adult.

CHAPTER 10:
CHILD PORNOGRAPHY AND SEX RINGS

Two other facets of child molestation that require attention are the uses of children in pornography, and the involvement of children in organized sex rings. The former raises Constitutional issues over the legal definition of obscenity and the First Amendment right of free speech, while the latter typically creates problems in investigation, prosecution, and the treatment of children.

Child Pornography

484. Baker, C.D. "Preying on Playgrounds." **Pepperdine Law Review,** 5: 809-852, 1978.
  Child pornography began appearing under the counter in adult bookstores in the late 1960's and by a decade later, was a flourishing, multimillion dollar business. Attempts to use traditional antiobscenity statutes and laws to regulate child pornography have been unsuccessful; it is recommended that these cases be tried under child abuse laws, and that federal statutes be passed to outlaw the production and dissemination of child pornography.

485. Doek, J.E. "Child Pornography and Legislation in the Netherlands." **Child Abuse and Neglect,** 9(3): 411-412, 1985.
  Because of changes in the laws relating to public morality, the Netherlands has become known as a country in which the production and distribution of child pornography occur without criminal penalty. This article reviews the history of some recent changes in legislation, most notably Bill 15836, which makes the production, distribution, exhibition, and transportation of child pornography a crime.

486. Massey, D.C. "No First Amendment Protection for the Sexploitation of Children." **Loyola Law Review,** 29(1): 227-235, Winter 1983.
  This paper reviews various state court decisions regarding child pornography.

129

487. Pierce, R.L. "Child Pornography: A Hidden Dimension of Child Abuse." **Child Abuse and Neglect**, 8(3): 483-493, 1984.

Child pornography may involve anywhere from 300,000 to 600,000 children nationwide every year. Although there is a general consensus that runaway children are the most vulnerable to the financial reward of appearing in pornography, other children are at risk as well. The longterm effects of this involvement on the children have not yet been determined.

488. Schoettle, U.C. "Child Exploitation: A Study of Child Pornography." **Journal of the American Academy of Child Psychiatry**, 19(2): 289-299, Spring 1980.

The case of a 12 year old girl whose sexual acts with other children and with adults were photographed and filmed is presented. The child came from a chaotically disorganized family, was of low average intelligence, and described feelings of helplessness, anxiety, and depression after her involvement with the pornography was disclosed. Therapy proceeded in three stages: dealing with feelings of guilt, anxiety, and loss of self-esteem; resolving the problems in the parent-child relationship; and resuming the normal developmental process.

489. Schoettle, U.C. "Treatment of the Child Pornography Patient." **American Journal of Psychiatry**, 137(9): 1109-1110, September 1980.

Therapy with a 12 year old girl who had been involved in a child pornography ring in which she was photographed in sexual acts with other children and with adults is described. Therapy proceeded in three stages: dealing with overwhelming and often immobilizing feelings; addressing problems in the parent-child relationship; and finally integrating the child back into a normal lifestyle.

490. Stack, E.J. "Preventing the Sexual Exploitation of Children: The New York Experience." **New York State Bar Journal**, 56(2): 11-18, February 1984.

In 1982, the United States Supreme Court upheld the constitutionality of the *New York v. Ferber* case which proscribed the promotion and distribution of material depicting children under sixteen in sexual activities, whether the material was legally obscene or not. The development of this legislation and the impact it has had since the Supreme Court decision are outlined.

491. Tyler, R.P. and Stone, L.E. "Child Pornography: Perpetuating the Sexual Victimization of Children." **Child Abuse and Neglect**, 9(3): 313-318, 1985.

Child pornography, the pictorial description of children in sexually explicit poses and acts, is a multibillion dollar business in this country which exploits anwhere from thousands to hundreds of thousands of children each year. Child pornography is viewed as a technique that perpetuates the sexual victimization of children since it typically becomes part of the collections of child molesters and because it both entices the children to engage in similar behavior, and is used to blackmail the children into continuing the sexual behavior. Various legal strategies for its control are described.

Sex Rings

492. Burgess, A.W.; Groth, A.N.; and McCausland, M.P. "Child Sex Initiation Rings." **American Journal of Orthopsychiatry,** 51(1): 110-119, January 1981.

Child sex rings are characterized by at least one adult who is simultaneously sexually involved with several children, all of whom are aware of each other's participation. The rings vary in organizational structure and may involve the production, collection, and trading of pornographic pictures of the children involved in the ring. An examination of 36 children involved in one of six different rings shows that the children are made fully aware at the onset of their involvement that sexual activity is a condition of membership, but their own sexual initiation typically begins with indirect approaches. Secrecy is paramount for the continuation of the ring and the pressure for secrecy is placed on the children by the adult and by their peers. The children are frequently symptomatic during their involvement with the ring and especially upon its disclosure. The reactions of the parents to the discovery of their children's involvement are also discussed.

493. Burgess, A.W.; Hartman, C.R.; McCausland, M.P.; and Powers, P. "Response Patterns of Children and Adolescents Exploited Through Sex Rings and Pornography." **American Journal of Psychiatry,** 141(5): 656-662, May 1984.

Three types of child sex rings are described: the solo ring involves one adult with a small group of children; the syndicated ring involves several adults in a well structured operation with many children that may also involve the children in pornography; and the transitional ring may involve one or more adults with several children in a loosely organized structure. An analysis of the involvement of 66 children in these types of rings reveals that each had been subjected to an elaborate socialization process that enticed them into the ring, coerced their cooperation, and assured their secrecy. Interviews with the children after the rings had been exposed reveal that they show various patterns of responses to their experiences: some have mastered their anxiety by integrating the event; some have sealed off their anxiety by denying the experience occurred; some demonstrated a repetition of symptoms indicative of chronic post-traumatic stress disorder; and others have introjected their anxiety and have identified with their exploiter.

CHAPTER 11:
THE PREVENTION OF CHILD MOLESTATION

With the emergence of child molestation as a social problem, strategies for its prevention have become popular in virtually every community in this country. Most of these strategies are designed for young children, teaching them personal safety, a good-bad touch continuum, the permission to say no to an adult, and the necessity of telling a trusted person if they are approached in some threatening or confusing way by another person.

If their popularity is any indication of their usefulness, then these prevention programs are indeed helpful. The following references, however, go beyond the intuitive appeal of such prevention strategies and examine not only the variety of prevention programs available, but also empirically evaluate their success in helping to teach children concepts and behaviors that will prevent sexual molestation.

494. Borkin, J. and Frank, L. "Sexual Abuse Prevention for Preschoolers: A Pilot Program." **Child Welfare,** 65(1): 75-82, January/February 1986.

A pilot project aimed at the primary prevention and early detection of sexual abuse among preschool children is described. Through the use of a puppet show, the children are taught the concepts of private zones of the body, the difference between good and bad touch, the permission to say no to sexual advances, the importance of trusting their feelings, and the need to tell a trusted adult if sexually approached by someone. A six week followup shows that 4 and 5 year olds have the best retention of information, with 43% of these children able to spontaneously recall the rules taught; only 4% of the 3 year olds are able to do so, suggesting that children that age may have to be taught with different techniques.

495. Comfort, R. L. "Sex, Strangers, and Safety." **Child Welfare,** 64(5): 541-545, September/October 1985.

Teaching children about the realities of sexual abuse and the skills needed to prevent it must be done in ways that are commensurate with the level of development of the child.

496. Conte, J.R.; Rosen, C.; Saperstein, L.; and Shermack, R. "An Evaluation of a Program to Prevent the Sexual Victimization of Young Children." **Child Abuse and Neglect,** 9(3): 319-328, 1985.

Although child sexual abuse prevention programs vary, they usually have elements in common: the concept of body ownership, a touching continuum, a discussion about secrecy, permission to trust one's own instincts and to say no, and the recognition of support systems. This study evaluates one such program as it was taught by a trained sheriff's deputy to 40 children, ages four through ten. The program was presented three consecutive days for one hour a day. Pre- and post-program questionnaire results show that both the younger and older children learned prevention concepts, although the older children learned slightly more. While this increase in knowledge is significant, the children as a group failed to learn more than half of the concepts the program is designed to teach. Data obtained from reviewing types of training show there is a tendency for the presenter to deviate from the model by placing more emphasis on the dangers that strangers pose and by using more "horror" stories than was intended in the model. The evaluation is encouraging and shows that children can learn prevention concepts, but it is also necessary to evaluate the program each time it is presented.

497. Fine, S. "The Teaching and Service Components of a University Sexual Medicine Clinic For Children." **Child Psychiatry and Human Development,** 14(1): 30-36, Fall 1983.

Data from cases referred to a university child sexual medicine clinic are used to teach medical students about the rate of occurrence, the clinical dynamics, and the basic prevention strategies for child molestation and incest.

498. Gilguin, J.F. and Gordon, S. "Sex Education and the Prevention of Child Sexual Abuse." **Journal of Sex Education and Therapy,** 11(1): 46-52, Spring/Summer, 1985.

Two major problems of child sexual abuse prevention programs are that they are not specific enough and that they overlook the role of the offender. It is important that children learn the proper names of body parts, and, because the offender can overwhelm even a well-prepared child, prevention programs also should be designed to teach identified child molesters the necessary controls to inhibit their own behavior. By also presenting programs on preventing sexually abusive behavior and attitudes in general, primary prevention can be guaranteed as well.

499. Kraizer, S.K. "Rethinking Prevention." **Child Abuse and Neglect,** 10(2): 259-261, 1986.

Most prevention programs evolve from a standard and largely unchallenged set of assumptions about what children know, how they think, and what they have to know. Although well intentioned, some of these programs unintentionally raise the anxiety and fear level of the children by teaching inappropriate and nonhelpful information. To be really successful, these programs must be designed for the developmental level of the children, must teach skills that can be reinforced throughout their lives, and must be reflective of the dynamics of child molestation.

500. Krugman, R.D. "Preventing Sexual Abuse of Children in Day Care: Whose Problem Is It Anyway?" **Pediatrics,** 75(6): 1150-1151, June 1985.

The recent flurry of legislation to mandate criminal and background checks and fingerprinting of potential day care employees is of questionable value in preventing the sexual molestation of children in that kind of setting. It is suggested that the pediatrician assume a leadership role in teaching parents how to recognize symptoms of anxiety and stress in their children, in explaining to them the indicators of sexual molestation, and in advocating for a national policy that encourages day care in the workplace.

501. McNab, W.L. "Staying Alive: A Mini-Unit on Child Molestation Prevention for Elementary School Children." **Journal of School Health,** 55(6): 226-229, August 1985.

A unit for teaching elementary school children protection from child molestation, incest, abduction, and involvement in pornography and prostitution is described.

502. Poche, C.; Brouwer, R.; and Swearingen, M. "Teaching Self-Protection to Young Children." **Journal of Applied Behavior Analysis,** 14(2): 169-176, Summer 1981.

The purpose of this study is to develop and evaluate a program to teach preschool children appropriate verbal and behavioral self-protection skills. Three children were each approached by an experimenter who engaged them in conversation and then attempted to lure them off of the grounds of the school by promises of a "surprise" in the car; each child responded positively to the lures. The children were then taught verbal and behavioral self-protective skills through modeling, behavioral rehearsal, and social reinforcement. Replications of the approach by the experimenter were rejected by the children both verbally and behaviorally, indicating that they had learned the necessary self-protection skills. Positive results continue into the third month, although it is recommended that children be given "booster" sessions to reinforce their learning at three month intervals.

503. Ray, J. and Dietzel, M. "Teaching Child Sexual Abuse Prevention." **School Social Work Journal,** 9(2): 100-108, Spring 1985.

A pilot sexual abuse prevention program for third graders in Spokane, Washington is described. The children viewed a slide show on "good touch" and "bad touch," watched the movie, "Who Do You Tell?" and engaged in discussions about personal safety with trained adults. A six month followup reveals that the children have learned and retained the relevant prevention issues taught in the program.

504. Robertson, K.E. and Wilson-Walker, J.A. "A Program for Preventing Sexual Abuse of Children." **American Journal of Maternal/Child Nursing,** 10(2): 100-102, March/April 1985.

A community-based sexual abuse prevention program that is aimed towards educating parents, teachers, and children about the realities of sexual abuse and the techniques and skills for its prevention is described.

505. Swift, C. "The Prevention of Child Sexual Abuse: Focus on the Perpetrator." **Journal of Clinical Child Psychology**, 8(2): 133-136, Summer 1979.

The prevention of child sexual abuse begins with understanding two things about the molesters: they usually have experienced sexual molestation themselves as children, and they are sexually ignorant. Case studies and references from the literature support these two hypotheses. Prevention, then, must incorporate prompt therapeutic intervention with sexually molested boys, and public education about sex in general and sexual molestation in particular.

506. Wolfe, D.A.; MacPherson, T.; Blount, R.; and Wolfe, V.V. "Evaluation of a Brief Intervention For Educating School Children in Awareness of Physical and Sexual Abuse." **Child Abuse and Neglect,** 10(1): 85-92, 1986.

Physical and sexual abuse prevention programs tend to have five objectives in common: teaching children that even someone they love and trust may punish them too severely or may involve them in activities that feel uncomfortable; children may experience anger, embarrassment, or fear when this happens; children should tell someone; the activities that do occur are not the fault of the children; and children should get help right away. This study looks at the impact of a physical and sexual abuse prevention program on 145 children, ages nine through twelve; results are compared to those of a control group of an equal number of children. After completing a pre-test questionnaire on these five issues, the children were exposed to two five-minute plays of simulated abuse experiences, followed by an hour long discussion session with a trained adult. A post-test questionnaire was administered three to five days later. Results show that children exposed to the prevention program give more correct responses to the items on the post-test questionnaire than do the other children, are more likely to trust their feelings about an incident, and are more likely to seek help from a trusted adult. What the study cannot measure is the impact this prevention program has on the behavior of the children.

CHAPTER 12:
PEDOPHILE GROUPS

The more sexually liberal atmosphere of the 1960's and 1970's in this country was conducive to the development of several pedophile groups that have agitated for changes in the laws that prohibit adult sexual behavior with children. Based on more successful and politically active pedophile groups in Europe, including the Pedophile Information Exchange (PIE) in England and the Pedophile Workgroup in the Netherlands, the three most prominent organizations in this country have had a limited impact on laws or on society in general.

The Rene Guyon Society, created in 1962 by a small group of parents after attending a conference on sexuality, took its name from a French jurist and Freudian psychologist who had been an outspoken advocate of adult-child sex. It also adopted his motto as its slogan: "Sex by year eight or else it's too late." The Society champions the abolition of statutory rape laws so parents can give their consent for their children to engage in sexual behavior with adults.

The Childhood Sensuality Circle was established in 1971 for the purpose of promoting sexual self-determination for adults and children. Believing that affection often overlooks age differences, the Circle advocates the abolition of the age of consent laws and encourages children to use their own standards in the selection of adult sexual partners.

The most politically active of the American pedophile groups, the North American Man/Boy Love Association was formed in reaction to the arrests of twenty-four Revere, Massachusetts men for sexual activity with adolescent males. Promoting an end to what it refers to as the state's repression of sexuality, NAMBLA also champions the abolition of all age of consent laws and works for the release of men incarcerated or hospitalized for noncoercive sex with children.

The following references use samples of subjects from one or more of these pedophile organizations, or examine the goals and impact on these groups.

507. Bernard, F. "An Enquiry Among a Group of Pedophiles." **Journal of Sex Research,** 11(3): 242-255, August 1975.

Seventy-three members of the Pedophile Workgroup, a pedophile organization in the Netherlands, were interviewed as to the development and nature of their sexual contacts with children. The majority of the pedophiles state they were first aware of their sexual attraction to children when they were between ten and twenty years old, and most had their first sexual contact with children during that period. Most state that they are attracted to pubescent children, although 39% state a preference for children under the age of eleven years. Boys are the sexual choice of 96% of the respondents; none shows a preference for girls only, but the remaining 4% prefer both girls and boys. Over half of the pedophiles reveal they have had sexual contacts with under fifty different children in their lifetime. Most of the pedophiles collect pictures or drawings of children and frequently exchange them with other pedophiles. Criminal convictions for their sexual behavior were experienced by more than half of the respondents, most of whom also had been psychiatrically evaluated and/or treated. When asked if they would eliminate their pedophile tendencies if given the opportunity, 90% state they would not change.

508. Brongersma, E. "Aggression Against Pedophiles." **International Journal of Law and Psychiatry,** 7(1): 79-87, 1984.

Interviews with members of the Pedophile Workgroup in the Netherlands reveal that a significant percentage have been personally victimized by people who espouse a prejudice or even blatant hatred against them as individuals and against their sexual preference in general. The origins of such hatred are examined and concerns about how such prejudices can be institutionalized within the law are discussed.

509. deYoung, M. "Ethics and the 'Lunatic Fringe': The Case of Pedophile Organizations." **Human Organization,** 43(1): 72-74, Spring 1984.

The publications and newsletters of three American pedophile organizations, the Rene Guyon Society, the North American Man/Boy Love Association, and the Childhood Sensuality Circle, are analyzed. Special attention is placed on the techniques of creating a pro-child ideology, allying with pro-child organizations and causes, and placing limitations on the behavior of members that these groups use to create an "ethical code" in order to make their unpopular philosophy palatable and their members acceptable to larger society.

510. Finkelhor, D. "What's Wrong with Sex Between Adults and Children?" **American Journal of Orthopsychiatry,** 49(4): 692-697, October 1979.

Intuitive arguments against sex between adults and children include the argument that it is intrinsically wrong from a biological and/or psychological point of view; that it entails the premature sexualization of children; and that it is damaging to the children. Each argument has some validity, but each is also weak. A stronger and sounder line of reasoning for prohibiting such sexual contacts is that the fundamental conditions of consent cannot prevail because children lack the two components essential to voluntary consent: knowledge to make them completely informed, and the freedom to say no to an adult.

511. Sandfort, T.G. "Sex in Pedophiliac Relationships: An Empirical Investigation Among a Nonrepresentative Group of Boys." **Journal of Sex Research,** 20(2): 123-142, May 1984.

Twenty-five boys who have on-going, mutually agreed upon sexual relationships with adult males who are members of the Pedophile Workgroup in the Netherlands, participated in a structured interview which utilizes a Self-Confrontation Method that determines what is important for the person at a certain moment in his life, and gives insights into the meaning of these events and feelings. All of the boys indicate a positive reaction to their sexual relationship with the pedophile, and all believe that the relationship has had a beneficial impact on their well-being. Although concerns about being discovered and punished did surface in the interviews, all of the boys state that the pedophiles' attention to them, their respect of their feelings, and their friendship far outweigh the disadvantages of such relationships.

The following references are literature reviews on narrow topics with-

in the general subject of child molestation.

512. Araji, S. and Finkelhor, D. "Explanations of Pedophilia: Review of Empirical Research." **Bulletin of the American Academy of Psychiatry and the Law,** 13(1): 17-37, 1985.

The empirical literature on pedophilia is reviewed and four themes emerge: the emotional congruence of the sexual act with the needs of the pedophile, his sexual arousal to children, his lack of legitimate alternatives for gratifying his sexual arousal, and his disinhibition through the uses of pornography and/or alcohol.

513. Bagley, C. "Childhood Sexuality and the Sexual Abuse of Children: A Review of the Monograph Literature 1978 to 1982." **Journal of Child Care,** 1(3): 105-127, January 1983.

The relevant literature on all types of child sexual abuse is reviewed.

514. Berlin, F.S. and Meinecke, C.F. "Treatment of Sex Offenders with Antiandrogen Medication: Conceptualization, Review of Treatment Modalities, and Preliminary Findings." **American Journal of Psychiatry,** 138(5): 601-607, May 1981.

The rationale for treating sexual offenders medically rather than punitively is reviewed. Special emphasis is focused on the use of antiandrogen drugs such as medroxyprogesterone acetate (Depo-Provera) which the literature shows has demonstrated success in reducing deviant sexual arousal and behavior.

515. Browne, A. and Finkelhor, D. "Impact of Child Sexual Abuse: A Review of Research." **Psychological Bulletin,** 99(1): 66-77, January 1986.

The empirical data as to the effects of sexual molestation on children are reviewed and analyzed. Methodological problems are pointed out, and the lack of empirical support for commonly held assumptions about the effects of child molestation are discussed.

516. Freund, K; Heasman, G.A.; and Roper, V. "Results of the Main Studies on Sexual Offenses Against Children and Pubescents." **Canadian Journal of Criminology,** 24(4): 387-397, October 1982.

The literature of child molestation and on incest is reviewed.

517. Frude, N. "The Sexual Nature of Sexual Abuse: A Review of the Literature." **Child Abuse and Neglect,** 6: 211-223, 1982.

In recent years, an adult's motivation to sexually abuse children has been redefined in terms of the need for power and the expression of aggression. This literature review examines the sexual motivation behind child molestation.

518. Jones, G.P. "The Social Study of Pederasty: In Search of a Literature Base: An Annotated Bibliography of Sources in English." **Journal of Homosexuality,** 8(1): 61-94, Fall 1982.

Pederasty is defined as an intimate sexual and social relationship of an on-going nature between an adult male and a young boy. This bibliography contains references to articles, books, and studies on pederasty.

519. Kilman, P.R.; Sabalis, R.F.; Gearing, M.L.; Bukstel, L.H.; and Scovern, A.W. "The Treatment of Sexual Paraphilia: A Review of the Outcome Research." **Journal of Sex Research,** 18(3): 193-252, August 1982.

Data of the treatment of deviant sexual behavior and the methodologies used in the studies are reviewed. Despite methodological shortcomings, almost all of the studies demonstrate positive results.

520. Lanyon, R.I. "Theory and Treatment in Child Molestation." **Journal of Consulting and Clinical Psychology,** 54(2): 176-182, April 1986.

The descriptive literature of child molestation is reviewed, with special attention to theoretical considerations and treatment strategies.

521. Mrazek, P.B. "Annotation: Sexual Abuse of Children." **Journal of Child Psychology and Psychiatry,** 21(1): 91-95, January 1980.

A working clinical definition of child molestation must include: an explicit description of the nature of the sexual act, its frequency, and whether is was accompanied by violence or threats of violence; information about the age, developmental and intellectual levels of the participants; a description of the relationship between the child and the adult; and an examination of the attitudes of the participants, the family members, and the prevailing culture. The literature is reviewed to show these definitional problems.

522. Mrazek, P.B. "Bibliography of Books on Child Sexual Abuse." **Child Abuse and Neglect,** 7(2): 247-249, 1983.

A list of forty-four books on the general topic of child sexual abuse, and a list of fourteen other books with chapters or selections pertinent to the topic are presented.

523. Newton, D.E. "Homosexual Behavior and Child Molestation: A Review of the Evidence." **Adolescence,** 13(49): 29-43, Spring 1978.

The intent of this paper is to review the research on the possible relationship between homosexual behavior and child molestation. Although methodological problems exist in the designs of studies in this area, a review of the literature shows that there is nothing more than a random connection between homosexuality and child molestation, despite the public's view to the contrary.

524. Quinsey, V.L. "The Assessment and Treatment of Child Molesters: A Review." **Canadian Psychological Review,** 18(3): 204-220, July 1977.

The relevant literature since 1960 on the treatment and assessment of child molesters is reviewed.

525. Rossman, G. P. "Literature on Pederasty." **Journal of Sex Research,** 9(4): 307-312, November 1973.

Various literary sources of information, including diaries, autobiographies, and memoirs on pederasty are reviewed.

526. Ryan, G. "Annotated Bibliography: Adolescent Perpetrators of Sexual Molestation of Children." **Child Abuse and Neglect,** 10(1): 125-131, 1986.

The literature on the characteristics, dynamics, and family issues as they relate to adolescents who sexually molest young children is reviewed.

527. Schultz, L.G. "The Sexual Abuse of Children and Minors: A Bibliography." **Child Welfare,** 58(3): 147-163, March 1979.

An extensive bibliography that is divided into sections on the history of child molestation, sexual development in children, interviewing techniques with molested children, the dynamics of molestation, incest, sexual exploitation, rape, treatment, prevention, the law, and the courts is presented.

CHAPTER 14:
BOOKS ON CHILD MOLESTATION

The last decade has witnessed an explosion of books published on the topic of child sexual abuse. Many books on domestic violence, family dynamics, and child abuse and neglect, to name a few, have excellent chapters or sections on child molestation as it is defined for the purposes of this bibliography, but the following books deal entirely or largely with the subject.

528. Ageton, S.S. **Sexual Assault Among Adolescents.** Lexington, Massachusetts: Lexington Books, 1983.
  A statistical study of the incidence and prevalence of sexual assault among adolescents.

529. Bass, E. and Thornton, L. (Eds.). **I Never Told Anyone: Writings By Women Survivors of Child Sexual Abuse**. New York: Harper and Row, 1983.
  First person accounts in both story and poetry form of child molestation by women who had experienced it are presented.

530. Bell, A.P. and Hall, C.S. **The Personality of Child Molester.** Chicago, Illinois: Atherton, Inc. 1981.
  A study of the psychosexual development of an incarcerated child molester through an analysis of over a thousand of his dreams combined with both biological and clinical data.

531. Burgess, A.W.; Groth, A.N.; Holmstrom, L.L.; and Sgroi, S.M. **Sexual Assault of Children and Adolescents**. Lexington, Massachusetts: D.C. Heath, 1978.
  A collection of articles on all aspects of child molestation with special focus on its dynamics, effects, and treatment approaches.

532. Burgess, A.W. **Child Pornography and Sex Rings.** Lexington, Massachusetts: D.C. Heath, 1984.
  A collection of articles on the uses of children in pornography and sex rings.

533. Conte, J.R. and Shore, D.A. (Eds). **Social Work and Child Sexual Abuse.** New York: Haworth Press, 1982.

A collection of articles covering the whole spectrum of child molestation with special emphasis on the treatment of the child, the family, and the child molester.

534. Cook, M. and Howells, K. (Eds). **Adult Sexual Interest in Children.** New York: Academic Press, 1981.

A collection of clinically focused articles on child molestation and incest.

535. deYoung, M. **The Sexual Victimization of Children.** Jefferson, North Carolina: McFarland, 1982.

A study of child molestation and of incest, with special reference to the dynamics, effects, and sociohistorical context.

536. Finkelhor, D. **Sexually Victimized Children.** New York: The Free Press, 1979.

Results of a survey with questions about childhood sexual experiences with adults and children, incestuous sexual experiences, and coercive sexual experiences at any age which was administered to 796 New England college and university students are presented. The literature also is reviewed to support the conclusions.

537. Finkelhor, D. **Child Sexual Abuse: New Theory and Research.** New York: The Free Press, 1985.

An examination of child sexual abuse from a social, moral and psychological perspective. The dynamics of the child molesters, the preconditions for his or her behavior, and the nature of the child at risk for being sexually molested are presented.

538. Finkelhor, D. **A Sourcebook on Child Sexual Abuse.** Beverly Hills, California: Sage Publications, 1986.

Five main topics: the prevalence of child sexual abuse, children at high risk, offenders, effects, and treatment are presented. The book reviews findings from community surveys and reviews the literature.

539. Geiser, R.L. **Hidden Victims: The Sexual Abuse of Children.** Boston, Massachusetts: Beacon Press, 1979.

All types of child sexual abuse, from incest, to child molestation, to the sexual exploitation of children in pornography and prostitution are discussed.

540. Groth, A.N. **Anatomical Drawings.** Newton Center, Massachusetts: Forensic Mental Health Associates, 1984.

A set of anatomically correct drawings of children, adolescents, and adults is provided and the use of these drawings in the investigation and treatment of cases of child molestation is discussed.

541. Holder, W.M. (Ed.). **Sexual Abuse of Children: Implications for Treatment.** Englewood, Colorado: American Humane Association, 1980.
A collection of articles on child molestation and incest, with special reference to the treatment of sexually abused children.

542. Kempe, R.S. and Kempe, C.H. **The Common Secret: Sexual Abuse of Children and Adolescents.** New York: W.H. Freeman, 1984.
The definition, evaluation, and treatment of incest and child molestation are described.

543. Knopp, F.H. **Retraining Adult Sexual Offenders: Methods and Models.** Syracuse, New York: Safer Society Press, 1984.
The nature of sexual offenses, with special reference to those that are directed against children, and the many myths that surround that behavior are discussed. Twelve successful treatment programs throughout the country are also presented.

544. Linedecker, C.L. **Children In Chains.** New York: Everest House, 1981.
An examination of the sexual exploitation of children by prostitution, pornography, and sex rings by an investigative journalist.

545. MacFarlane, K., and Waterman, J. **Sexual Abuse of Young Children: Evaluation and Treatment.** New York: Guilford Press, 1986.
The sexual abuse of preschoolers, their assessement, evaluation, and treatment are presented.

546. Mayer, A. **Sexual Abuse: Causes, Consequences and Treatment of Incestuous and Pedophilic Acts.** Holmes Beach, Florida: Learning Publications, 1985.
The dynamics and treatment of both incest and child molestation are presented.

547. Mohr, J.W.; Turner, R.E.; and Jerry, M.B. **Pedophilia and Exhibitionism.** Toronto, Canada: University of Toronto Press, 1964.
A clinical study of two types of sexual deviations, pedophilia and exhibitionism is presented.

548. Mrazek, P.B. and Kempe, C.H. **Sexually Abused Children and Their Families.** New York: Pergamon Press, 1981.
A mutidisciplinary and multicultural approach to the sexual abuse of children is presented.

549. O'Brien, S. **Child Pornography.** Dubuque, Iowa: Kendall Hunt, 1983.
The nature and extent of the uses of children in pornography are discussed.

550. O'Carroll, T. **Paedophilia: The Radical Case.** Boston, Massachusetts: Allison Publications, 1982.

A defense of pedophilia by one of the founders of the Pedophile Information Exchange (PIE) in England, an activist group for men sexually attracted to young boys.

551. Plummer, C. **Preventing Sexual Abuse: Activities and Strategies for Those Working with Children and Adolescents.** Holmes Beach, Florida: Learning Publications, 1985.

A sourcebook on prevention strategies.

552. Rossman, P. **Sexual Experiences Between Men and Boys.** New York: Association Press, 1976.

An examination of pederasty and the pederasty underground in this country.

553. Rush, F. **The Best Kept Secret.** Englewood Cliffs, New Jersey: Prentice Hall, 1980.

Social, religious, and political patterns throughout history that have been conducive to the sexual victimization of children are analyzed from a feminist perspective.

554. Russell, D.E.H. **Sexual Exploitation: Rape, Child Sexual Abuse, and Workplace Harassment.** Beverly Hills, California: Sage, 1984.

An examination of several types of sexual exploitation, including child sexual molestation.

555. Sandfort, L.T. **The Silent Children: A Parent's Guide to the Prevention of Child Sexual Abuse.** New York: McGraw-Hill, 1980.

Written for parents and professionals, this book examines the motives and circumstances of all types of sexual abuse of children. Prevention and education strategies also are stressed.

556. Schultz, L.G. (Editor). **The Sexual Victimology of Youth.** Springfield, Illinois: Charles C. Thomas, 1980.

A collection of articles covering the legal control of child sexual abuse, and its diagnosis and treatment.

557. Sgroi, S.M. **Handbook of Clinical Intervention in Child Sexual Abuse.** Lexington, Massachusetts: D.C. Heath, 1985.

A series of articles on the diagnosis, evaluation, and treatment of sexually victimized children and their families.

CHAPTER 15:
CONCLUSION

This review of the literature has demonstrated a number of important facets of the study of child molestation. First, a variety of methodological approaches can be, and have been, used. From case studies of molesters and children, to retrospective record reviews, to theoretical approaches, to empirical studies, the published references on child molestation have created a rich and varied look at a complex phenomenon. Methodological problems abound, to be sure, and inconsistent conclusions can be found in the literature, and while there is much to be said about the development of sound empirical studies on this topic, the fact remains that child molestation can be examined from a variety of different perspectives, and that each has the potential of increasing our knowledge.

Second, it is obvious from this review that the study of child molestation is not the exclusive domain of any one discipline. Literature from psychology, sociology, medicine, law, and a host of other disciplines examine this topic. The possibility of an interdisciplinary study of child molestation holds great promise for an even more thorough and comprehensive look at this behavior and its effects on children.

Finally, what is an unsettling but perhaps inevitable conclusion of such a review of the literature is that gaps in knowledge become even more glaringly obvious, and what is not known about child molestation seems at times to exceed what is known. That reality, however, need not be taken as defeat; it can, instead, motivate and stimulate more research on this subject, more interdisciplinary attention to it, and more commitment to the topic as a viable and important subject of examination.

An undertow of skepticism is beginning to tug below the wave of recent enthusiasm about recognizing child molestation as a social problem. There are those who say the attention now given to it is nothing more than a fad, a passing fancy that surely will be supplanted by another, perhaps more tragic and dramatic, social problem. Historically, there is some analogous evidence that would seem to support that skepticism; we as a society have attended to a variety of social problems, from poverty

146

to serial murders to the homeless, with great enthusiasm and concern at different times, only to find that months or years later, the problem seems to have magically disappeared only because we are no longer attending to it. That may happen with child molestation as well. But even if the "fancy" passes, this behavior, which has been a feature of every culture and each generation, will continue. The knowledge that is accumulated now, and the current commitment to research on this subject, will help us continue to deal with the human dimension of this problem long after society's collective attention has turned in another direction.

AUTHOR INDEX

TITLE INDEX

SUBJECT INDEX

171